Womankind

FACES *of* CHANGE AROUND *the* WORLD

text by Donna Nebenzahl   *photographs by* Nance Ackerman

The Feminist Press at the City University of New York

New York

Published in the United States in 2003 by The Feminist Press
at the City University of New York. The Graduate Center,
365 Fifth Avenue, Suite 5406, New York, NY 10016
feministpress.org

This book was created and published by Raincoast Books
9050 Shaughnessy Street, Vancouver, British Columbia, Canada V5P 6E5
www.raincoast.com

Raincoast Books acknowledges the ongoing financial support of the
Government of Canada through The Canada Council for the Arts and
the Book Publishing Industry Development Program (BPIDP); and the
Government of British Columbia through the BC Arts Council.

Edited by Lynn Henry
Jacket and text design by Val Speidel

LIBRARY OF CONGRESS CONTROL NUMBER: 2002091841

Printed in Hong Kong, China

10 9 8 7 6 5 4 3 2 1

In memory of Anita Borg
1949-2003

I dedicate this book to the strength and wisdom of the women in my life, from the past, present and future . . .

To my grandmothers Marie Louise and Ida
To my mother, Pam
And to my daughter, Hannah Wakerenhawi

— Nance

In memory of my Portuguese grandparents, whose good care and hard work were an inspiration, whose fierce love helped me forge my path.

— Donna

Contents

vii

"We will meet,
All of us Women, of every land
We will meet in the center, make a circle
We will weave a world web
to entangle the powers
that bury our Children."

— excerpted from a poem in "Sing a Battle Song: Poems by Women in the
Weather Underground," 1975, author unknown

Introduction

THIS IS A TRAVELLERS' TALE. IT'S a story of discovery and adventure, of long months of planning that crystallized into encounters of great joy and moments of unbearable sadness. We are the travellers, but ours is not a travel book. We have voyaged around the world, but in the *favelas* of Brazil or among the high rises of Hong Kong we have been searching for something altogether different from a sense of place.

At the other end of the flight, the train trip or the bus ride, we've been trying to get to the heart of why women care. We know women care; they are mothers, after all, and they comprise the majority of the caring professions. But why, we asked ourselves, do they care enough to dedicate their lives to helping others?

So we chose to meet some of these women, a handful among the thousands and tens of thousands who spend their days and often their nights among the poor and the innocent, struggling to protect or improve, to pull out of harm's way or simply to put food on the table for the millions in need.

They are fighting for the power to do this. Aware that knowledge is power, they seek intellectual or spiritual rights. Because solidarity is power, they struggle to create effective coalitions. Knowing that freedom is power, they labour to ensure that a woman or child will not be used by others.

To find them, we lobbied caring organizations, talked to friends and colleagues, consulted those in the field, and came up with a list of women — some local, some international, most well known within their community and others known around the world. They work for children, for human rights, the environment, for small farmers and women in high tech, for the injured and oppressed.

We have had some experience doing this. Nearly a decade ago, my friend and colleague Nance Ackerman and our newspaper's designer Louise Vincent started working with me on a women's daybook we titled *Portraits*. At that time, I was editor of a section at *The Gazette* in Montreal, Canada, that focused on women's issues. It seemed a natural adjunct to this work that we produce a daybook that would highlight the women of Quebec. Nance did the photography and I interviewed a dozen women, among them the inspiring Dr. Lucille Teasdale who, by the time that agenda was published, had died of AIDS contracted while she performed surgery in Africa. I remember interviewing her, already frail but speaking firmly, at a flat in east-end Montreal. I asked her, what did it mean to her, knowing that she was suffering from this fatal disease? "We all have to die of something," she answered simply.

When we began in 1993, we didn't know that the first agenda would lead to five more years' collaboration, the last three doubling the number of women

1

photographed and interviewed and expanding across Canada. By 1998, Nance had moved back to Nova Scotia with her two young children to be near her family and the ocean she loved. And we were tired out trying to produce the agendas as well as finance and market them.

We decided to call it quits, but I would occasionally joke to Nance that now that we had covered Canada, all we had left to do was the world! It was a passing notion — until the great millennium discussion took place. Why don't we try it, we reasoned. After all, activist women of the world would be a perfect millennium project.

The Canada Council for the Arts, our funding body, agreed. They had supported a previous project of Nance's on native women of Canada, and they must have been pleased. In the summer of 1999, the project won a Millennium Arts Grant, the first of a jumble of funding — private, corporate and public — we were to receive so we could document, in words and photographs, the work and lives of activist women. We knew early on that the book would be called Womankind, a title that conjures up both a woman's place in the world and her sense of compassion.

Nance and I, mothers of school-age children, did not tackle this project for the excitement of seeing the world. While Nance has had her share of adventure — photographic trips to Lebanon during the war, to Guatemala for the Smithsonian, a pre-children fling with skydiving — and I had spent enough time in Europe to know I could trek with a pack on my back, we both understood the project would take time and place real demands on our families. So we tried as best we could to organize our time away around soccer championships, concerts, dance competitions, exams; in short, all the paraphernalia of our lives.

We began to see that we had come to this place in our personal journeys because something intrigued and captivated us about women who choose to care, and fight. More than that, they also choose to believe that they can make a difference. We knew that this drive and optimism was shared by women around the world, and perhaps because of our own fractured cultural baggage, we were determined to explore it. After all, what better subject for a feminist journalist who was born in South America of Portuguese and English, possibly Polish parentage and a feminist photographer of Mohawk, Scottish and German extraction?

In truth, the worlds we were seeking were not out there, in the geography of the place. They were in the minds and hearts of the women we hoped to meet. Why did they choose to face such difficulties? What gave them the courage to keep going?

It turned out that they were as unalike as people could be, the way a Buddhist scholar would differ from an Andean elder or a Nigerian chief from a Russian feminist. But in many ways they were bound by the same sweep of determination and courage. The compassion that shone from the eyes of Tina Chery in Dorchester, Massachusetts, whose fight against violence is done in the name of her murdered teenage son, is mirrored in Enakshi Thukral's hands clasped around the grimy fingers of Delhi slum children. The resoluteness in the gaze of Nawal el Saadawi,

2

determined to expose the anti-feminist constraints of Islam, finds reflection in the steely countenance of Emily Lau, trying to bring democracy to the people of Hong Kong.

From the beginning of our travels, when we trudged through the rustling cornfields of the valley of Chontala in Guatemala to meet with the women weavers and listened to Sebastiana Pantó Pox tell the story of a life unravelled by civil war, we understood that we had been given an incalculable honour. The women in this book have shared with us their lives, their sorrows and hopes and, in many cases, the great joy and energy that seems to glow from within. We have had a chance here — and this is something we think about often — to witness the ways ordinary people are moved to do extraordinary things.

The more we travelled, the more we struggled with rising to the occasion. I mulled over words while Nance agonized over the right moment, light and setting for her photographs. Even after she has connected with her subject, captured the laughter between gypsy activist Ágnes Daróczi and her mother, or the resolute sadness in the stature of Vancouver breast-cancer survivors, Nance keeps on thinking of how to do it better. We have sifted through photos, laboured over nuances in the writing, discussing, sometimes arguing, but always reaching a place that gives us satisfaction. Both professionals with many years' experience, Nance and I have come to realize the value of our combined effort, of the chance to share a glimpse of an extraordinary woman captured on two distinctive levels, in a moment in time. We would like the pages of this book to be experienced this way: look at the photograph, study her face and her surroundings, then read the story of her journey to this place where we have all met. If we've done our work as we hoped, you can then look at the photograph again, and really see her eyes, or the sweep of her arms, in a new and different light.

We know that while a book is real and finite, women's lives are always changing. Since we travelled to South America to start our work in November 1999, Nawal el Saadawi was forced to fight an Islamic demand that she divorce her Muslim husband because she preaches equality for women. Françoise David has left the helm of the Quebec Women's Federation. And Adriana Hoffman took a government position only to return to her forest advocacy work. But whatever course the lives of activists take, we believe that certain truths will stand the test of time.

We found these things to be true. That activist women often come to their work out of sadness and despair, because of personal loss, but sometimes simply out of deep conviction that something has to be done. That they have boundless energy, and shoulder on in the face of all the difficulties because of a certainty in their mission. That technology has provided an unsurpassed connection with the world, which has been a source of real support. Finally, and significantly, that caring gives them hope — despite the hunger, displacement and ecological devastation — that they can change the world.

Donna Nebenzahl / Montreal, Canada / February 2002

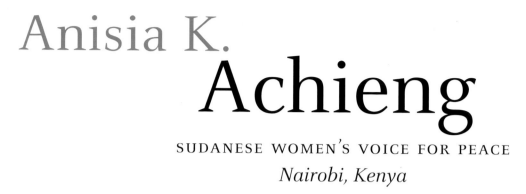

Anisia K. Achieng

SUDANESE WOMEN'S VOICE FOR PEACE

Nairobi, Kenya

EVERY WOMAN IN SUDAN HAS EXPERIENCED THE EFFECTS OF WAR, SAYS Anisia Achieng. For seventeen years, a civil war that has received only a smattering of attention from the rest of the world has been raging in her country. It continues to this day — the longest ongoing civil war in the world, in which an estimated 1.9 million people from southern Sudan and the Nuba Mountains have lost their lives.

Anisia lived in the Nuba mountains, an area particularly hard-hit by the government military and the Sudanese People's Liberation Army. Over the years, more than four million southern Sudanese have been forced to flee their homes — a figure so gigantic that the claim to posterity of this deadly war is that it has produced more internally displaced people than any other war on earth. Anisia had been working with the internally displaced, but in 1993 she was forced to run when the rebels and the army entered Nuba and killed many thousands of people.

5

Anisia's two young children, just twelve months and six years old, had escaped with her sister into the bush and, aided by the Red Cross, had walked to Uganda. Anisia tried to escape by going to Khartoum, spent nine harrowing hours at the airport and was finally airlifted out on a military plane with the wounded. Her husband, who later abandoned the family, was studying in London.

In Nairobi, she met with other Sudanese women who had escaped. In March 1994, six of them sat down to talk about their own complicity in the conflict. "We feel that women are marginalized," says Anisia, who has the slender build and graceful height of many Sudanese. When the group numbered twelve women with different backgrounds, they decided that the only way to be effective was to find ways to resolve the conflict. The task they uphold is to promote dialogue, "unified as women, not caught up behind husbands."

In Sudan, the root cause of conflict is not just religious and economic, it is political, Anisia says. For forty-five years, the use of force has brought catastrophe to the country. Non-violence is needed, so the Sudanese Women's Voice for Peace invited political groups — twenty-nine men — to the table and listened to them. Then they presented their concept, their dream of peace.

With help from Unifem at the United Nations, they evaluated their position and took their findings to the 1996 United Nation's conference on women in Beijing. "Our work showed the conflict was political," Anisia says. "The government has not been faithful to its people."

Now they have set about building peace with a role for women, without whom there is nobody. "Every man and woman came out of a woman," Anisia says. "We do not want to lose our husbands and children; we want dialogue. We want to know the root cause, to understand why we are victims of war." The group has been talking for seven years, sometimes aggressively. They have gone to women, the wives of warlords and commanders, and asked: "Are you happy if your husband is killing your brother?"

They also do community peace-building and conflict-resolution training in three regions in the Sudan, including Anisia's southern home in the Nuba

Mountains. They have trained more than sixty women to promote peace and conciliation at the community level and have built five peace centres, which are part of the Seeds for Peace program they started in 1998. Now, with more than 500 members and a lot of partners outside who are committed to their mission, Anisia believes that "if you threaten with truth, people will benefit." Nevertheless, she despairs of the men who don't want to accept the forgiveness being offered them.

Reunited with her children after two years, Anisia, who is thirty-five and descended from a royal line, spends most of her time travelling and working for peace in the Sudan. Not being with her children has made her strong, she says. She is familiar with orphaned children, having been one herself: her father died when she was not yet born, her mother just a year later as she tried to help out a neighbour in a domestic violence dispute. She was given to missionaries by her grandfather and received her education with their help.

Being orphaned means you're standing with other children, she says. She has special interest in the plight of tens of thousands of Sudanese orphans who are there, all alone.

Anisia has concluded that war is not just war, it's also economic gain. In the Horn of Africa, she says, look at the trafficking of girls and women. Having understood all these things, she knows that when the conflict has ended, she and her peacemaking partners have certain plans.

"If all the girls were to go to school," she reflects, "then the world would be in peace."

"We sat down and asked ourselves, 'Why are we silent? Can women be peacemakers?'"

Georgina Ashworth

WOMEN'S RIGHTS ACTIVIST, FOUNDER OF CHANGE
Chiddingfold, Surrey, Britain

GEORGINA ASHWORTH IS COMFORTABLY ENSCONCED IN A PICTURE-BOOK English village. Her fourteenth-century home is an homage to early days in that ancient land. But don't mistake this middle-aged woman, who offers cups of tea and cake to visitors, for a dowager who putters in her garden and puts up jams for the village fair.

She might enjoy both activities, but Georgina has other things on her mind. She has spent her life examining the way governments and civic leaders have ignored women and she has no intention, more than twenty years later, of changing her ways. In 1979 she created Change, one of the first women's rights NGOs in the world, and in the process shamed those governments into doing more.

Georgina Ashworth

*"There is still the **tendency** to say it doesn't matter, man or woman, the world is the same. They're denying if you leave home in the morning and you're a woman, life is different."*

When she began working in human rights in the 1960s, Georgina understood the Universal Declaration of Human Rights stated that people have the right to live without fear and hunger. What she saw, however, were millions of women who lived in fear and hunger every day of their lives. She read publications about minority groups all over the world; their focus was always on men. Women were invisible, she says.

Her position was international, natural for someone who had been brought up in Spain, Egypt and Greece. The human-rights group she created decided to issue written reports on women's situation country by country, an innovative approach at the time. Their second report, on prostitution in Thailand, attracted the attention of the Council of Europe and the United Nations.

Change reported on more than two dozen countries, and along the way lobbied the British government to create working groups in advance of UN conferences on women that would link different sectors of government. Her weapons were intelligence, an ability to shame — and her wit. "I used to joke," she says, "that the British delegation consisted of a Baroness, two Dames and three men called Richard."

But by the time she attended the non-governmental meetings at the UN Conference on Women in Nairobi in 1985, the largest gathering of women in the history of the UN, she could see people grow and understand. At last, she was part of a worldwide movement.

Georgina, who learned the importance of handing over her good ideas, points out that now Britain has a women's unit in government. She made more inroads and by the late 1980s Change was working in Brussels to begin putting gender in trade and aid, another unusual concept. It didn't stop there: she launched the Women's Alternative Budget Group, using academics and volunteers to critique the U.K. budget from a gender perspective. Now, she says, the idea of analyzing budgets in this manner has spread and is being advocated by the UN.

By the 1990s, Georgina's reports were being done farther afield, at the request of the European Union. Uganda, Madagascar, Botswana, Namibia, Sierra Leone, Guyana, Fiji, Guinea-Bissau, Cape Verde, all were covered. Change gave lobby training in Zimbabwe, Ghana, Jordan and Eritrea.

Now Georgina wants Change to create "good governance" reports, pointing out the gains women's movements have made around the world. By describing what has been done, she wants to shame into action those who have done less. The reports, she says, will be "a mixture of celebrating what's been achieved and lessening the isolation of those not in the networks."

Through the years, Georgina has wielded her independence like a standard, ignoring backlash and criticism, and carrying on. It's very sad, she says, that people can't see there's a cause for which others are prepared to strive. Women's liberation is her cause, in all its complexity. "I get overwhelmed," she admits, "but I'm good at bringing everything together. I tend to see all the connections."

The good governance reports will portray how those connections interrelate. She will, for instance, discuss economics because while human rights are supposed to guarantee freedom from hunger, economics — which is about budgets, not people — can violate human rights. And economic reality is quite different when you see it through women's eyes.

Angela
Bailón Pérez

POVERTY ACTIVIST
Guatemala City, Guatemala

A FULL MOON HANGS IN THE SKY OVER GUATEMALA CITY. IT OVERLOOKS THE twinkling lights of La Esperanza, a squatters' settlement that clings and spreads on the hillsides at the city's edge. It beams over the dusty roads, cooking fires by the sidewalks, over the petty crime and grinding poverty. It shines gently even as ragged children wander the streets or gangs of thieves board buses and rob the captive passengers.

Angela Bailón Pérez grew up here. She is forty and has spent a lifetime with addiction and despair. The daughter of alcoholic parents, she is married to an alcoholic. Mother of two boys and a girl, she is a high-cheekboned beauty but for her dark eyes, reddened by the grit of her surroundings.

Angela
Bailón Pérez

It was because of her children that Angela took the first step along a path that brings her, this warm night under the light of the full moon, to a sturdy stucco building at a crossroads in the settlement. This is where she learned that her life could be transformed, where she found the solace and support that would change her forever.

"I had a second child and my husband is an alcoholic," she says. "I couldn't live. Here I felt cared for and loved." She began working at UPAVIM, a cooperative that offers job training, tutoring, medical services and support to poor women. She began by sewing in the craft program, content to earn less than she would at factory work if she could be in the company of other women. In the ten years since, Angela has learned and grown, has worked at a desk and used a computer. A quiet woman, she was overcome with emotion when the others chose her to head the cooperative.

She knows the only way out of the stifling poverty here is to keep on working, to help the children fulfill their dreams. Angela believes in education, is determined to support her eldest son, who wants to become a doctor. "I don't know how," she says, "but if he wants that, we will try to do it."

Growing up with nothing besides the hopelessness of the ghetto, she has clambered out of its darkness. Her accomplishments are the light she shines on her life. She is showing her children by her own good work that they can do the same.

14

"I don't want my daughter to have a life like I lived. It's very sad for me and the children to live with an alcoholic man. I tell her I made a mistake. She must study and have a different kind of life."

Emma
Bonino

POLITICAL ACTIVIST

Rome, Italy

EMMA BONINO KNOWS REPRESSION WHEN SHE SEES IT. IN 1998, AS EUROPEAN Parliament minister for humanitarian aid, she became involved in a campaign to help women living under Taliban rule in Afghanistan. She was visiting a group of women health workers there, and was amazed to see that when the women took off their veils, they were heavily made up.

"They were doctors and teachers," she says, chatting between calls and a dozen interruptions as she stretches out behind her desk at the offices of Italy's Radical Party. "Makeup was for them a way to resist, a way to feel real." The Taliban were furious to discover that the group had photographed the women, and Bonino and her entourage were held at gunpoint for four hours. "I saw there," she says, her English tinged with the beautiful cadence of her native language, "a blatant violation of human rights."

Emma Bonino

Now, in the wake of September 11, Bonino's work in the European Parliament is even more pressing — the ratification of the international criminal court treaty, an effort that finally bore fruit in July of 2002. The concept, she says, is like the land-mines treaty: to have member states establish a criminal court to judge crimes against humanity. It's a step forward from an ad hoc tribunal established only after genocide, which makes a point but has little deterrent value.

Now you will be judged; your impunity is finished. "Look at Milosevic," she says. "It's the first time a living guy cannot travel or escape. Look at Pinochet, he might escape but he cannot win the next election. Nothing is more fragile than dictatorships."

She may be considered a criminal by the Taliban, but Bonino is judged by many to be an honest and erudite politician. When she was given the North-South Prize in 1999, Hans-Peter Furrer of the Council of Europe spoke of her role as European Commissioner and the "spirit and personal courage" she showed when "exposing the violations of human rights and shaking the conscience of those who are apparently good-willed but more than often just idle and indifferent . . ."

She may be diminutive and conservatively dressed, but Bonino has never been idle. Her life of activism started at the University of Milan in Italy, where she graduated with a degree in foreign languages in 1972. By 1975 she had given up teaching to become president of the Radical Party. She was elected in 1976 to the Italian House of Representatives; by 1978 abortion was legal in Italy. She was elected to the European Parliament in 1979, where she was appointed Human Rights Commissioner and travelled to some of the most dangerous parts of the world, such as Rwanda and Kosovo.

In her decades in politics, Bonino has built a reputation as a skilful political player who honed the radical edge she displayed at her first mass action in the 1970s. "It was a turning point in my life," she says. She was twenty-seven at the time, and pregnant by a man who had told her he was sterile. Forced to undergo a clandestine abortion after one doctor she visited refused the procedure unless she paid him one million lire, she was humiliated by the experience, and spoke to many other women who felt the same way.

"I was shocked," Bonino says. "I am a good citizen." So she and her friends organized a centre of civil disobedience, helping women have abortions. The more the women gathered, the more outraged and vocal they became. Before long, they were arrested, and Emma Bonino's political career was launched. She has never looked back.

For her, the rights and responsibilities of individuals is key. In Italy, she believes politicians don't stand squarely behind their positions in the face of the power of the Church. There's a difference, she argues, between belief and laws. "What my country thought and now thinks," she says, "is that a sin is a crime."

Known as a courageous street fighter, this most effective communicator believes that dialogue must constantly be fostered between the public and institutions. "But you must have a lot of fantasy also, to attract the media," she says with a laugh, "like spending five days and nights sitting in front of a government building, so people wouldn't forget to vote in the referendum!"

"However the tools may change, the basic idea is always the same: **to take responsibility, to communicate what you are doing, to speak the truth."**

19

Anita
Borg

TECHNOLOGY ACTIVIST

Palo Alto, California, U.S.A.

ANITA BORG, BAREFOOT AND IN JEANS, WEARS A T-SHIRT THAT SAYS "Well-behaved women rarely make history." The kerchief around her head covers a scar, the remnant of surgery to remove a brain tumour that has quieted, but only briefly, this effervescent woman who stands at the vanguard of a new movement, one that is demanding women's say in technology.

Involved in a milieu that is heavily academic and notoriously focused, Anita nevertheless rode motorcycles, renovated houses and learned to paddle kayaks, all the while earning a place in the world of technology with a PhD from New York University in 1981. People kept telling her she couldn't do it that way. "I told them," she says, " 'Look, I'm going to have some fun.' " And she has.

Radical women approach the world differently, and Anita Borg wants women in technology to be radical. We can't deny technology, she says, we have to embrace it. It took her a while to figure out how.

At a conference for research about operating systems in 1987, attended by only about twenty-seven women out of 400 participants, Anita ran into a friend in the women's washroom. They chatted, and soon there were six or seven women talking in the tiny bathroom. She suggested they all sit together at dinner.

All but two women came, and during the evening she took their e-mail addresses so she could contact them about the website she soon created, dedicated to women in technology. She called it Systers. Membership soon grew from that small group to one hundred women, and today there are twenty-five hundred to three thousand women in thirty-eight countries. The rule, says Anita (who for years was called "her systers' keeper"), is to discuss the intersection of technology and women.

But she knew that wasn't enough. "The way tech is created 'for women' is to come up with stuff and try to sell it or have focus groups," she says. "Nobody ever gets women together talking about what their life is about and have *them* creating the stuff." To that end, she has given talks and organized technology conferences that attracted hundreds of top-notch women. But the pinnacle of her radicalism is her Institute for Women in Technology.

Now, as she travels all around the world, Anita is sure that something new is happening. She has gone to developing countries and met with hundreds of women, insisting that they not simply accept the technology derived from the West. It must be something you create, she tells them.

She wants the Institute to explore new ideas, so she brought together technology specialists and other women, on an equal footing, to brainstorm. The idea, she says, is to talk about family and community and how technology could help. Now, thirty to thirty-five women meet here in Silicon Valley — some technical women, others housewives, career women, students — in a model called a thinking environment. "They start talking about the future," Anita says. "They come up with lists of what might be important. In two days, hundreds of wild ideas are distilled to six or eight."

One idea was "smart plumbing," a computer system to indicate if a building's plumbing is about to freeze or break. Another was the virtual wall, that goes up like wallpaper and connects rooms in other houses with your own wall, so it feels like you're in the same room. That way, grandparents could visit, Anita says.

Ideas like these drive a number of research issues, but are reflecting the needs of ordinary people. What women need, how women work, is at the centre of Anita's thinking.

"If it isn't our technology," Anita says, "we're screwed. We have to have control."

"My role is to empower women around technology to say, 'This is what I want.' Also to empower women who want to create technology to do what they want. Not have someone say, 'That's women's stuff. That's stupid.'"

Helen Caldicott

ANTI-NUCLEAR ACTIVIST
Victoria, Australia

SHE HAS BEEN CALLED THE MOST COMMITTED ACTIVIST IN THE WORLD, an impassioned proponent of peace and eloquent protestor against nuclear proliferation.

She paid for it with a broken marriage and the resentment of her children. But she spent her life the only way she could. "I had to," says Helen Caldicott. "I was impelled."

She is a tall, handsome woman, evangelical and unafraid, convinced that people must listen to her warnings about power, military and political. For more than thirty years, she has waged a war against nuclear proliferation, convinced of its dangers to humanity.

Helen Caldicott

It began in 1971, when she supported the Australian government's opposition to French atmospheric nuclear testing in the Pacific, and continued when she moved to the United States in 1977. A pediatrician specializing in cystic fibrosis, Dr. Caldicott left a teaching post at Harvard University Medical School in 1980 so she could devote her energies full time to the prevention of nuclear war. Since then, she has practised medicine for a time, only to return once more to the cause that drives her.

While in the United States, she founded the Women's Action for Nuclear Disarmament (WAND) and Physicians for Social Responsibility — doctors devoted to educating others about the danger of nuclear weapons. The international umbrella group, International Physicians for the Prevention of Nuclear War, won the Nobel Peace Prize in 1985.

Now living in Australia, she divides her time between writing and lecturing and heading the California-based Nuclear Policy Research Institute. The students she speaks to think they live in freedom, she says, "but they're not free psychologically. People have to know what the risks are. They have to know about the militarization of space. They need to know the status of the planet."

She has written books and countless articles, was nominated herself for the Nobel Peace Prize. One of the films in which she was a subject, *If You Love This Planet*, won the Academy Award for best documentary in 1983.

The movement was at its height during the Reagan years of the 1980s, when so much protest work was being done. Since then, she says, we've assumed that nuclear weapons would be destroyed and "we went back to our couches." But the U.S. Joint Chiefs of Staff nixed that idea: "We were threatening their family jewels," she says.

Dr. Caldicott believes that people must once again be mobilized, to counteract the extraordinary power of politicians. She points out that some U.S. government actions — removing themselves from the treaty on biological and chemical weapons and from the Kyoto Accords on the environment — have potentially frightening consequences.

When the planes hit the World Trade Centre on September 11, she was travelling across the United

States by Greyhound bus, speaking at universities. Your country is in grave danger, she told the students, but she can see that people are uniting under patriotism. "It appeals to the male primitive . . . it's tribalism," she says.

She speaks with tremendous force, trying to shock her listeners into understanding the state of the world. "What I hope to do is rupture their psychic plumbing."

In her early sixties, Helen Caldicott is still full of passion and ideas. She is convinced that her work and the work of others has prevented the use of nuclear arms — until now.

She despairs of America and mostly of how little its citizens understand what is happening there. The United States, she says, is potentially the most brutal nation in the world, and Americans "don't know what's being done in their name . . . by the psychotic men in power."

"The planet is terminally ill."

Nancy
Cardia

EDUCATOR, HUMAN RIGHTS ACTIVIST

São Paulo, Brazil

SHE BEGAN HER WORK AS A SOCIAL PSYCHOLOGIST, TRYING TO UNDERSTAND whether proposals made by architects and engineers would alleviate the housing problems of the poor. To do this, Nancy Cardia left her university office and spoke to the people living in the barrios and squatters' settlements of São Paulo. Then in the early 1980s, democracy began to take hold in Brazil, and she started to see that it could sustain movements that would help the slum-dwellers and the disenfranchised.

The housing question could not be solved until people made demands, she realized, and they must learn to do this. But how do people learn in a country where children don't go to school, she wondered. These very people, the ones who must demand rights, fear those in authority; they become hostage to two sides, police and criminals. Their poverty tarnishes every element of their lives.

28

She has heard the rich complaining about ragged children at play, demanding they go back to their slum homes. If a woman argues about the health-care service, she will be insulted as uneducated. The stigma of being poor denies the poor access to rights.

In such an unequal society, people at the top are not questioned, she says. Are they entitled? No one asks. People blame themselves for their own future, never the institutions or structures. Poor education is acceptable for poor children.

For Nancy Cardia, the continuing violation of human rights means power relations are not changing. She knows that many poor people can't really voice their needs or wishes. A tall, straight-talking intellectual, she leads the Institute for Human Rights from her small office at the University of São Paulo. She faces a difficult question, one that impacts the poor of this massive city: How can you implement human rights here?

Impunity is a great force behind the violence, she says, so the police as much as the criminals get away with murder. Her institute has investigated cases in São Paulo, looking at all the court proceedings, analyzing the behaviour of judges, police and prosecutors. They have interviewed people, analyzed press clippings, reconstructed cases, used the Penal Investigation Code to observe how police officers worked.

What they found, she says, was appalling. Evidence was lost; people were wrongly accused.

More than once, she has cursed herself for having the idea, for thinking that the result of all this work would foster justice. In spite of the progress toward democracy, violence and violation of the right to life is rampant in São Paulo. Out of despair, society supports lynching, death squads. This is the violence that the state perpetuates.

Often, she feels criticized and reviled. She also feels respected. Because of the work at the Institute, people have been forced to look at the violence, at the abrogation of human rights. She feels hopeful when, sometimes, even the police want the Institute's interpretations and solutions.

"The police are not here to break the law. They are here to enforce the law and *if they don't,* that threatens democracy. I tell them this.

For some reason, it's something they don't wish to hear."

Clementina Chery

PEACE ACTIVIST
Dorchester, Massachusetts, U.S.A.

HIS NAME WAS LOUIS BROWN. HE WAS A TALL, GOOD-LOOKING FIFTEEN-YEAR-old, an honour student who aspired to become the first black president of the United States.

A few days before Christmas, on December 20, 1993, Louis Brown was on his way to an afternoon Christmas party for Teens Against Gang Violence, a group he had joined just months earlier. He left his home in Dorchester, a haven for the boy who stayed in a lot to avoid the mean streets, and walked toward the local train station. Minutes later, as he was entering the ramp of the station, he was caught in a gang shootout. A bullet to the head ended his young life.

Louis' mother, Clementina Chery, has gone over those last moments many times: how she fed him his favourite meal, fried chicken and mashed potatoes; how she thought to drive him, as her husband Joseph usually did, to and from school because of the dangers. But her licence had expired. "I tell myself," she says sadly, "there's nothing I could have done."

Now in the clapboard house on that quiet street, there is a locked room. But Louis' legacy is more than a memorial, a boy's life frozen in time. When their son died, Clementina and Joseph felt they were being asked to do something. They wanted to find a way to honour Louis, to use his story to help other young people realize their dreams. So they created the Louis D. Brown Peace Curriculum, using literature and young people's initiatives to explore the good that can be accomplished.

"Kids hear all the time 'you can't,'" says Clementina, dark eyes flashing, her youthful countenance in stark contrast to the emotional burden she carries. Many of these kids are heads of households, have dealt with trauma, seen friends, siblings, cut down at a young age. One of the kids in Grade Ten dedicated an essay to seven of his friends who were murdered. No wonder so many have lost hope.

Sometimes, Clementina wants to give up. "But I have a bundle of letters," she says. "I sit here by myself, and I begin to read those letters, thanking me for giving them hope, for sharing Louis, for letting them speak about their loss and pain." Her eyes fill with tears as she stares out the window, remembering.

Knowing the nightmare herself, Clementina has begun a program for family members of homicide victims. Your whole world comes crashing down, she says, but there's a connection if people hear from someone who knows what they're going through. "I am that someone who will reach out to help you out of the ditch."

The pain and loss will never go away. Nor will her anger, that her son was murdered in daylight, that the system doesn't help those who must live with violence. But the most important decision is what to do with that anger.

"What would Louis do?" Clementina asks herself sometimes, as she sits in that locked room surrounded by her precious boy's books and clothes. "Then I hear him say, 'You're doing okay, Mom.'" This is how she heals.

"I know Louis is guiding me. I know this is not us, not our work. This is his work. He never got a chance to show what he could contribute. It's up to us to use his life, our pain and anger, to make a difference."

Katsi Cook

NATIVE HEALER, ACTIVIST
Ithaca, New York, U.S.A.

KATSI COOK IS A GRANDMOTHER, HEALER, MIDWIFE, DREAMER, A WOMAN who believes in the traditional ways. Longhouse people, she says, are keeping ceremony alive from the old days, when there was maple water to drink, peyote medicine. When you can't relate to the environment, you're losing spiritually.

Katsi is also a free thinker. She likes the idea of many creators, of exposure to many indigenous medicines. It's her job to respect medicine ways. "I'm in this world," she says, "wondering, 'How does it work?' I have to be open minded."

37

Katsi Cook

"We're fighting so the next generation of midwives can have the best of both worlds."

She is bathing her grandson in the kitchen sink. The little boy, sparkling dark eyes and tousled hair, succumbs to his beloved grandmother's washing. This is the baby who was nearly lost at birth, she says, and for days and days she cried for him. His name, Omadweyaashk, means "the sound of the water when you're standing by the shore."

Katsi Cook has a pealing laugh, an open face, a big heart. "I tell people," she says, "if it wasn't for the Mohawk, Jacques Cartier wouldn't have survived." The French explorer and his men were welcomed and cured of hunger and scurvy by the people of Akwesasne.

She loves midwifery, but loves it more when it's magical. For twenty years, she has gone to births. She brings dreams to her work, stories of the old ways. Once you bring birth back into the home, she says, you bring ceremony back. A woman has to know some connection with the earth, so part of Katsi's research as a midwife is to grow corn; it takes a lot of nurturing. Women have instinctual keys, she believes, and the midwife's job is to find those keys. This whole universe is a mother.

She works in the world of spirits — a world like this one, she says, but without dimension. She wants to know how we think, authentically. She wants to see this old well of knowledge survive.

What she sees now are families recovering from stress. "If your grandma was sent to a residential school," she says, "you can be sure you're affected by it." Katsi sees casinos and taxes and smuggling. She sees in her midwifery many women who lack an ability to be intimate.

"We're fighting," she says, "so the next generation of midwives can have the best of both worlds." Just like the corn is growing, women are growing, and a day of awakening will come. She looks for messages in every event, finds them often in dreams. One dreamscape has stayed with her for decades. She tells it as native storytellers have often told about their world, using ancient symbols — turtle, stars, buckskin.

"It was June 9, 1984 and I had done about three home births. I dreamed I was sleeping in a treehouse. An old woman with a black shawl comes up the ladder and tries to warn me. I don't want to wake up. I go down the ladder and behind the house are huge cornfields that slope to a lake. In the middle of the night, stars shining like diamonds, translucence lifting up into the lake, I see women with black shawls and I realize they are doing something. I am running now. I see stars spinning and they take the shape of a turtle, they take the shape of a spinning spiral, a circle. I get high as the stars, they are toward me in a line. They turn into Iroquois women in calico and beads. The first three women, I know them. I'm wearing white buckskin.

"All of a sudden, I woke up. I didn't want to leave the dream. It was like ecstasy."

Ágnes Daróczi

ROMA WOMEN'S ACTIVIST
Budapest, Hungary

KATA BARSONY IS SEVENTEEN. SHE IS A DARK-HAIRED, dark-eyed Roma girl, and because of her gypsy heritage it is unusual in this country that she is in university.

It becomes clear why Kata has broken the mould. When Kata's mother, Ágnes Daróczi, was seventeen, she was the first ever to speak the Romany language on Hungarian television. Years later, Ágnes organized the first Roma art exhibition at the Cultural Institute of Hungary, where she worked. Through her life, she has done many things to bring into the light a culture that had been trampled and hidden away.

But the place of Roma people in this society is not assured. Most live in poverty. More than seventy percent are unemployed, many in the small villages. In Hungary, like elsewhere in eastern Europe, the first people who lose jobs are the Roma, many of whom are unskilled and uneducated. Most Roma children are placed in "special schools," segregated from other students.

And why? Capitalism has come to Hungary, but in the so-called capitalism, Ágnes says, the Roma haven't any capital.

Ágnes grew up in a small village, 240 kilometres from Budapest, peacefully learning the Romany language at school along with Hungarian and Russian. After grade eight, although the secondary school was sixty kilometres from her home, her grandmother — her mother's mother — insisted she go, and she lived away from home through her high-school years. "Because of my parents we escaped," she says of herself and her four siblings. "They were strong enough to send me away to learn. It was hard for them, and for me. But they wanted a better life for their children."

Then she went to university. "Before I began

university," Ágnes says, "I entered an open competition in poetry and read my poem on television." It was the first time people had heard the Romany language on TV. "I wanted to show how big and beautiful is our culture."

She and her friends would sing Romany songs, and collect folklore. They would also organize cultural evenings for the Roma people who worked during the week in the city, staying in hostels. "This collection," she says proudly, "is now at the Academy of Science, recorded on more than forty CDs." They created a successful radio program about Roma literature, called "The Sound of Roma," and out of that came a folklore ensemble, Kalyi Jag, that went on to perform all over the world.

Ágnes began to work at the cultural institute in 1978, satisfied that she had been creating a cultural image to show Roma values. "We thought that was very important," she says, "because most of us forgot the power of self-knowledge, to be proud of ourselves as a nation."

When she was growing up, she says, no one spoke about the Roma nation or the minority except in a pejorative way. But when you look at the sweep of

Roma history, there is much to be proud of. "We are European," Ágnes says. "We live in a diaspora, in peace with the majority. We had great metalworkers, made guns, sabres and bells. We excelled in music, entertainment, culture. We were very well accepted."

But the twentieth century was hard for the Roma people. After the First World War, the factories were built, and instead of handmade goods there was a demand for factory-made. The Second World War brought forced assimilation — and the systematic annihilation of the Roma, the medical experiments by the Germans, beginning in 1938.

"The Roma were never people of writing," Ágnes says. "They moved around so people didn't know about them. They had been persecuted for so long that they were afraid to give names to their children."

Ágnes is not afraid. She has moved beyond purely cultural expression to develop a political Roma movement. At her mother's stucco house with its red tiled roof on the outskirts of Budapest, she shares jokes and shells peas with the old lady. "I sent my daughter to learn," Ágnes' mother says, "because I hadn't any chance to learn and I have a good head. Education is more important than money, because you can lose money but what you have in your head you always have."

In the walled garden, full of fruit trees and pole beans climbing up dried-out stalks of sunflowers, Ágnes explains the desires of the Roma and the role of the independent Roma association she helped create in 1990. "We want to live on the same level as others," she says, "but not forget our traditions. We want to educate our children to have jobs and houses, to become lawyers and doctors."

"My daughter is the only Roma child in her class. Ask her how many times she has felt prejudice."

Françoise
David

SOCIAL JUSTICE ACTIVIST
Montreal, Quebec, Canada

THEY BEGAN IN 2000. IN BURKINA FASSO ON 6 MAY, TEN THOUSAND WOMEN marched. In France on 17 June, another ten thousand. On 14 October, a women's rally in Brussels coordinated women from Eastern and Western Europe. On 15 October, the march in Washington, twenty thousand strong, passed in front of the offices of the International Monetary Fund. On 17 October, a group of women met United Nations Secretary General Kofi Annan.

Known as the World March of Women,

this international protest against poverty and violence against women was a marriage of local and global activism. It was also the culmination of years of organizing and hard work, the fruit of a seed that had been planted five years earlier.

Françoise David

*"We can do our struggles locally, but we have to do them **globally** as well."*

In March of 1995, the Fédération des Femmes du Québec (FFQ) organized an anti-poverty march from Montreal to Quebec City, several hundred kilometres along the north shore of the St. Lawrence River. They called it Bread and Roses and when the eight hundred marchers arrived in the province's capital city, they joined a rally of twenty thousand in front of the National Assembly.

Women from Africa and Latin America were on that march, and they encouraged Françoise David, head of the FFQ, to organize a second march like Bread and Roses, but on a world scale. At that time, the FFQ weren't part of any international network, and though David was concerned about her lack of experience in these matters, she decided to try. She had met many women at the UN women's conference in Beijing that year, and by the end of 1996 had sent letters and received responses from women's groups in forty countries.

It was a good idea at the right time, and so the World March of Women was born. By the time they had their first international meeting, a lead up to the World March, 145 delegates from sixty-five countries were involved, two-thirds from Asia, Africa and Latin America.

David has always been a leader, involved at school, at summer camp, an active participant in a family of six children. Her father, a doctor, founded the Montreal Cardiology Institute and her mother was a social justice activist and writer. At home, she says, the girls had the same education as the boys and all were taught to be just. "They told us we had great opportunity," David says, "and that we must respect the poor." Her mother, who died when David was twenty-one, encouraged her to be a social worker.

She worked in Rwanda, Uganda and Kenya and by the late 1980s was a community organizer at women's centres, believing them to be good ways to marry individual service and collective action. By 1994, she was named president of the FFQ, and in her steadfast, quiet way was credited with bringing visible minority women, lesbians, handicapped and the young into the organization. For her, there is no question whether her allegiance lies with the rich or poor. "I would always support the poor," she says.

She has realized, more and more, that businesses do what they want — she has awakened to the negative impact of globalization. "We have jobs locally, but if money goes to free-trade zones, we lose jobs," David says. "People there have jobs, but no protection." The women who marched, she knows, want to be part of a global solution.

A year later, the women involved in the March inscribed this mandate:

"We, women of the world . . . faced with the crucial stakes confronting humanity; faced with the unprecedented rise of poverty around the planet and all forms of violence against women; declare that we are more determined than ever to continue marching together, on all the continents, because we are convinced that another world is possible."

Leslie
deBeauvais

THEATRE OF HOPE FOR ABUSED WOMEN
Los Angeles, California, U.S.A.

LESLIE deBEAUVAIS KNOWS THE HEALING POWER OF THEATRE. DESPITE HER genteel appearance, the shoulder-length bob and pretty features, there is something world-weary about Leslie. She is a survivor of domestic violence and child abuse who learned through acting that it's possible for survivors to express pain and sorrow, anger and fear, the feelings of abandonment, the guilt. Theatre helps people heal, she says, "from the inside out."

She created a theatre program to do just that. Since 1996, the Theatre of Hope has been a dream come true for Leslie. She had studied acting as an adult, and felt it help her heal. Someday, she thought, I will use theatre to help the abused.

Steps away from a traffic-laden Los Angeles thoroughfare, the two small theatre spaces and adjacent courtyard are suffused with warmth and light. This is what Leslie, the executive director, wants the women and girls to feel, those who come to see or act in productions of the Theatre of Hope. Originally, the program offered staged readings to educate the public. Then word spread and the actors started taking readings to shelters, expanding the repertoire from domestic violence to child abuse. One of their productions — a drama in three vignettes called "Random Acts of Evil" — was used as a model for medical students to identify child abuse. Actors are often women in shelters or teenagers in detention centres or probation camps.

Leslie got involved in theatre arts when her two stepdaughters suggested she take an acting class. Coming to acting later in life, she discovered that it could "touch the core of one's being." Out of her past, the experiences she had put away, came those moments of abuse and violence. "I realized," she says, "that I was healing myself. I have two sons and it was

important for me that my sons know about my experience. With this program, I came out."

Violence in your life depletes self-esteem so much so that many children, Leslie says, have no idea why they're on this earth; it's a place full of fear and darkness, without joy. It's amazing when they start to do theatre, to watch them open up. "We're trying to help them understand that there's nothing wrong with them."

She is beginning now to work with youth at risk, in a program called "Writing on the Wall," doing theatre with girls in detention who are between the ages of ten and seventeen. Mask-making is a successful therapy these girls use, as do the women in the program. Masks can express how you feel today; they can be everything you've experienced and in some cases what you see in the future.

Leslie opens a box of masks, many decorated with sparkles, plumage and coloured feathers. One of the masks is black, with red-rimmed eyes, silver tears dripping and a thin, open mouth. It is a mask of despair: the woman who made it eventually committed suicide. Another has sparkles and tears. "Our tears are always part of us," she says. "We try to teach that every day is your choice."

It's a struggle to keep the theatre going with mostly volunteers and very little money. There are almost one hundred families who work through the project and nearly two hundred youth, learning body movement, script and music, how to crew, stage manage, light and act. Because of them, she says, "even if we don't have the money, we do it anyway."

This is truly her theatre of hope — for the future, for the children, for herself. "It's the best gift I have been given in my entire life."

"One of our group has a motto: 'There is no shit in this world. All the things that we experience, we compost and can use again.'"

Nawal
el Saadawi

TEACHER, WOMEN'S RIGHTS ACTIVIST
Cairo, Egypt

WHEN SHE RETURNS TO EGYPT, NAWAL EL SAADAWI TAKES COMFORT IN THE time she spends at Kafr Tahla, her father's village in the Nile Delta. There, surrounded by palm trees, fields and the winding river, she claims part of her lineage, the peasant family that gave her strength, the grandmother who sent all her children to university and, by raising the standards for her children's children, saved her. Nawal is a doctor, teacher, poet, novelist.

Now seventy, Nawal is a beautiful woman with a casual grace. Her thick white hair flies about her head, her slanting dark eyes sparkle with curiosity and intelligence. No longer practising medicine, she has turned her full attention to writing, teaching and to speaking out. In doing those things, she is unwaveringly courageous. Her subjects are the taboos of her society — women, sex and religion. She chooses them, she says, because the system is unfair, based on exploiting women and the poor. She has done so at great risk.

In 1972, she was imprisoned under the government of Anwar Sadat, lost her job. The magazine she edited linked poor health to poverty and was shut down; it was a threat to the governing elites. Her work was censored and she was forced into exile for almost a decade. With her great longing to expose the powers that ruin women's lives — the traditions of sacrifice and the veil that make young girls subservient to their husbands — Nawal forged ahead despite the forces aligned against her. She so angered the fundamentalist extremists that her name was on a death list from 1992 to 1997.

But Nawal continues to speak out, to rebel as she did as a child, when she questioned the way her family treated her compared to her own brother. "They told me, 'That's what God said.' So I rebelled against God!" Since then, she has never stopped writing, even through medical school. The result of Nawal's need to express herself is thirty-two books of fiction and non-fiction in Arabic; twenty-two of these have been translated into English and thirteen into Japanese.

Everything in her writing, she says, is political. Now she is organizing Arab women and teaching at universities in the United States. The veils, she tells women, don't just cover your faces; they shroud your minds also. Searching for truth whatever the cost, she warns students to beware of academia because it tends to ossify, to put you in a frame. Only creativity counts, she tells them. Creativity means breaking limits. "I am committed to justice, freedom and love," she says fiercely. "That is god to me."

Travelling the world, Nawal says she feels like a fish outside the sea when she is not in Egypt. But her greater ocean is politics, because for Nawal life is made of politics. Social and political action is her inspiration. After so many years and disappointments, she is as sure of this as she is of anything.

"Language, journalism, food, sex, all is politics. Even innocent love stories are political. When you have two people in a bedroom, that is political — who is above, who is below.

There is no such thing as neutrality."

Tahmeena
Faryal

REVOLUTIONARY ASSOCIATION OF WOMEN OF AFGHANISTAN
Karachi, Pakistan

FOR YEARS, SHE WAS KNOWN ONLY AS TREENA, AFRAID FOR HER LIFE BECAUSE she secretly helped women who lived in a country where they were rendered invisible. When we saw her, her face was in darkness, and she described what she had witnessed: shrouded women, some beaten for showing a wrist, others forced into prostitution or left to beg on the streets because they were not allowed to work.

Her real name is Tahmeena. She was born in 1978 in Afghanistan and went to school in Kabul. When Tahmeena was ten years old, her family fled to Pakistan, and there she began her work for the Revolutionary Association of Women of Afghanistan (RAWA), an organization devoted to helping women. All their projects were secret; the Taliban decreed that any member of RAWA who was caught would be stoned to death.

Tahmeena Faryal

Her role now, she says, is to speak for all the grief-stricken women of Afghanistan. She calls them "the largest forgotten tragedy on our planet."

Years of famine and depression made women too weak to care, she says. And the mental torture was incessant. In Afghanistan under the Taliban, a woman could not go to school, see a doctor or even a male tailor. Calling a woman by her name was forbidden, her shoes could not make noise. She had to darken her windows so she couldn't be seen.

"We expect nothing from people who shed the blood of innocents."

Now the Taliban is no longer in power but RAWA's mission remains the same. After all, Tahmeena says, Afghan women were dominated by the Northern Alliance from 1992 to 1996. They, too, are criminal and misogynist.

"By wearing neckties, they can't claim democracy," she says. "They are warlords, and as long as we have warlords we can't have democracy."

Under the Northern Alliance, there is no official restriction on education, but there's also no sense of safety or security. So women continue to wear the burka. These were the people, she remembers, who destroyed schools, museums and hospitals before the Taliban.

RAWA wants to bring knowledge to women — in a country where just five percent are literate — to show them that the key to freedom is to overthrow fundamentalism. Fundamentalism is the opposite of freedom, Tahmeena says. It cannot be cured.

RAWA fights for democracy, freedom, social justice. "We look for a democratic Afghanistan, and it's not hard to find democratic elements," Tahmeena says. But already under the Northern Alliance there are reports of rape and destruction in the country.

She is most disturbed by the mental destruction, the effect of more than two decades of war. In a few years, we might rebuild our country, she says, but almost everyone has been affected mentally because of the punishments they have endured day after day. Innocent people have been tortured.

She continues to hope that the international community will not support fundamentalists, although only after September 11 did people care about Afghanistan, despite RAWA's constant warnings.

The destruction of the Buddha statues, she remembers, got more coverage than the ongoing tragedy.

"It's very sad that the statues were destroyed," Tahmeena says, "but we can never compare statues with the blood of our people."

Jane Frost
and Brenda
Hochachka

DRAGON BOAT BREAST-CANCER ACTIVISTS
Vancouver, British Columbia, Canada

JANE FROST AND BRENDA HOCHACHKA ARE BOTH IN THEIR FIFTIES, BOTH mothers of three, both breast-cancer survivors, twice over. Both had small children when they were first diagnosed.

But they are bound by more than this. They are both dragon boaters. They wear fuchsia T-shirts that say "Abreast in a Boat." Their long, slender craft, resplendent with its dragon's head and tail, is launched regularly into the waterway at the local community centre for training runs.

61

Jane Frost and Brenda Hochachka

*"We realized our impact only after the first dragon boat festival. It became **a broader message of life** after breast cancer."*

What started out as an exercise program for women who had undergone breast surgery, to see whether this type of repetitive training might alleviate the associated soreness and swelling, has grown into a world movement. It has turned breast-cancer patients into athletes. Because, when these women take to their dragon boats, something magical happens.

Brenda and Jane embraced the magic, a welcome respite from the struggle to survive. Brenda was diagnosed in 1983 and had a second mastectomy in 1993. Jane's cancer resurfaced in her lung and bones after thirteen years.

After the first bout, Jane remembers trying to teach her young sons to do housekeeping. After the second, she sat with her boys to talk about her illness, knows that her mother and sister are here for them if she goes. Brenda's son, after her second treatment, shaved his head in empathy.

At the first dragon boat festival, there were twenty-four women in the boat, ranging in age from thirty-two to sixty-four. That event, attended by more than twenty-five teams from around the world, transformed those twenty-four women from cancer victims to dragon boaters. Even family members looked at them differently, Jane says. "We became new people."

They started to work out at the gym three times a week, and to get to know each other. One woman's depression lifted when she joined the team. "It's like a floating support group," Brenda says, "and we're all in the same boat!" There are now 125 dragon boaters in their group. At their first dragon boat festival, ten teams came from across Canada.

The women have discovered the joy of competition and the camaraderie of sport. Many women with breast cancer see them as messengers of hope. After the world festival in New Zealand in 1998, Jane says, a group of Maori sisters called them "strong and mighty women."

They are astonished, and pleased, that they've influenced people. Women handle this illness differently because all women are different, Jane says, but all seem to get what they need from the group. The greatest gift, the one that joins them all together, is to realize that they're more than breast-cancer survivors. They are fighters.

Enakshi
Ganguly Thukral

CHILDREN'S RIGHTS ACTIVIST
Delhi, India

MOTHERHOOD GALVANIZED ENAKSHI GANGULY THUKRAL, DELIVERED
her as naturally as childbirth from years in social work into a passionate advocacy for the rights of
children. In her rooftop office, just steps away from her comfortable apartment in a block of buildings
on the outskirts of Delhi, the thirty-something Enakshi can stop for a moment, away from the hustle
of street life where little children scavenge in rubbish heaps or spend long hours labouring in factories.

Her own beloved son and daughter, basking in their
parents' affections, playing and learning with childhood enthusiasm,
filled Enakshi with the strength to fight for those mites with dirty faces
and torn clothes who scrabble to survive in the alleys and on the
dumpsites of India.

64

Enakshi
Ganguly Thukral

Enakshi has many examples of how children are used in her country. Little street urchins massaging white men on the beaches of Goa. Boys who leave school for months at a time with an "uncle" and come back with money in their pockets. Eight-year-olds sent away to work, only to return battered and abused. Six-year-olds who can't go to school because they must look after babies and toddlers. Children under fourteen — at least twenty million of them — who work in industry, as domestic workers, in agriculture, at roadside stands.

What about these children? Who takes responsibility for them?

"Our sympathy and empathy are always with adults, who have a voice in a country with no social security and social stigmas galore. We say people with AIDS *have rights, but what about these kids?* **What about the children?"**

The government, says Enakshi, prohibits children from working in hazardous industries and regulates work hours in other industries. But by regulating, they are approving. Look at the children. Any employment that denies them their rights — to education, to the freedom of childhood — is hazardous, even if those hazards are not visible.

Her own life is full of joy — she has an accountant husband, two thriving pre-teens, good friends with successful careers. But no amount of personal comfort would deter Enakshi once she realized that even where children are protected, in government-run homes, they are not safe from harm. After the second death in a particular children's home, Enakshi — articulate, quick to laugh, equally at ease in a sari or jeans — decided to focus her activism solely on children.

She rankles at the injustice done to those who cannot speak for themselves. Should the state ban child labour, she points out, it would then be incumbent upon them to provide work for adults, schools that are accessible to all children, even girls, even those denied education because of caste. Unless you can let them be free, she says, children cannot go to school and they are doomed to repeat the cycle of poverty and hopelessness that consumes their parents.

Enakshi shares this anonymous poem:

I am the child.
All the world waits for my coming.
All the earth watches with interest to see what
I shall become.
Civilization hangs in the balance,
For what I am, the world of tomorrow will be.
I am the child.
You hold in your hand my destiny.
You determine, largely, whether I shall succeed
*   or fail;*
Give me, I pray you, these things that make for
*   happiness.*
Train me, I beg you, that I may be a blessing to
*   the world.*

Nathalie Geismar Bonnemains

LES MÈRES EN COLÈRE/ANGRY MOTHERS
Cherbourg, France

THEY LOOK BENEVOLENT ENOUGH, GREEN HILLS ON THE LANDSCAPE around the La Hague nuclear plant, the world's largest commercial facility to separate plutonium and uranium from spent nuclear fuel. But those pastoral-looking mounds are deadly; beneath them lies a stew of liquid and gaseous nuclear waste.

They are the reason, says Nathalie Geismar Bonnemains, why the children of Cherbourg are dying of infant leukemia and other cancers. She is part of Les Mères en Colère, a group of angry mothers who will not stop until that nuclear-waste facility is shut down.

Nathalie
Geismar Bonnemains

They are familiar with nuclear power; the plant has been there for thirty years, a monument in the landscape of a country that depends on reactors for eighty percent of its energy.

They had long suspected that their environment was being poisoned, and when the first study came out, suggesting a rise in leukemia cases among children playing near the water and eating local fish, Nathalie and one hundred other mothers felt their anger rising. "For my children," Nathalie says fiercely, for the toddler Titouan, six-year-old Martin and nine-year-old Manon, "I want the company to stop telling lies."

Nathalie grew up in this area; her parents and grandparents live in the community. She is small and hard-boned, so direct that it's only when she embraces her young daughter Manon that her tenderness shows. Until now, there has been silence on this issue, she says, because husbands work at the nuclear facility so wives don't speak.

But for this tough countrywoman, it's too late to be silent. In her group, she says, women do speak, and they're saying they want no more nuclear waste, no more poisoning of the environment. Her anger is even stronger since a more recent study confirmed the earlier findings of a leukemia cluster near La Hague.

The 1997 study, published in the *British Medical Journal* by epidemiologist Jean-François Viel, stirred the Mothers into action. He found an excess of children's leukemia in the district of Beaumont, within ten kilometres of the reprocessing plant — four cases where 1.4 would be expected. Some months later, two studies were set up at the request of the Ministry of Health and the Environment and their findings in July 2001 confirmed the earlier results. The study claimed that the cases found between 1978 and 1988 were 6.38 times greater than expected, a statistically significant figure.

For Nathalie and the Mothers, there is clearly a link between the illnesses and the mixing of radioactive and chemical pollution that has been seeping from La Hague. Activists report radiation leaks at the facility, and possible contamination from transports of nuclear waste being brought to La Hague.

Les Mères en Colère believe that the government-subsidized company is obliged to find a solution. They want regular checking of blood counts, studies on exposure, research on pollutants, a halt to the storage and reprocessing of spent fuel from foreign countries. Even though much of the country is alarmed, Nathalie worries that the company will do nothing. The corporation, Cogema, finally acknowledged concern but disputed the link between "operations at the Cogema-La Hague site and the probability of occurrence of infantile leukemia."

The network of Les Mères en Colère is more vigilant than ever, knowing that as time passes they represent the population's growing anxiety. "We are doing this for future generations," Nathalie says.

It is unlikely, though, that the company will ever find a way to transform those deadly mounds into true green hills.

*"In France there is a nuclear lobby to continue this, but also a conscience to change the way we use energy. **Little by little, people are demanding good energy.** For us, that is the objective of our work."*

Adriana Hoffman

DEFENDER OF THE FORESTS

Santiago, Chile

ADRIANA HOFFMAN TOOK AN ABANDONED QUARRY IN
the heart of Santiago and showered it with love. The stones were dragged
away, the ground turned and fed. Into its good earth she delivered growing things,
the native trees and plants of Chile.

Twenty years later, her garden on the hill covers five
hectares. She calls it Mapulemu, a native word meaning forest from the
earth, and it thrives despite the choking atmosphere of a city grown double
in size in six years. Children come and stand at a rocky outcrop overlooking
the lagoon, fascinated by the movements of the aquatic birds. Leaves rustle
in the wind, the sun warms the earth and Adriana is joyous.

Adriana Hoffman

Some of the trees growing here were near extinction, she says, touching the leaves of a towering palm, the first tree planted in Mapulemu. Knowing it like a lover, she is still amazed by the garden's beauty.

Her passions now take her on a greater quest, to defend all the native forests of Chile. She is a botanist, and wants to do more than write books and articles. She wants to save the trees, and her organization, Defenders of the Chilean Forests, is a lobbying force in the country. She believes the forest is the environment in microcosm: in its partnership with the ecosystem, it embraces organisms, soil, water, atmosphere.

Adriana tells the story of Chile before the Spanish, when more than half the country was covered with forests, only small bits taken by indigenous people whose harmony with the land could not save them when the invaders came. Then the forests were cleared for agriculture; the impact is a blight on what is dear to her. To recuperate the old-growth forests takes more time than we can imagine, she says. It takes centuries. She is determined to save what's left of the country's forests.

To do this she must fight the forestry companies, and economics and politics have loud voices here. Adriana ponders the terrible fate of those fine old trees, turned by commerce into wood chips for the Japanese market, replaced with fast-growing American pines and Australian eucalyptus. In her campaign to save them, full of emotion and values, she is looking for an advocate among the new political forces in the country.

She is being heard now, more than ever before, though her country's political adventures are well known. She is now a player among the intelligentsia in Santiago, a scientist from a family of scientists. Her parents, both doctors, were forces in the cultural life of the city. Her mother, she says, was a revolutionary woman who embraced women's issues in a profound and spiritual way.

There is something spiritual as well about Adriana as she works to preserve the forests, in the way she stands alongside the peeling bark of a molle, a native tree from the north. Her cheeks are pressed close, her hands caress the bark. She is full of patience and love. I can hear it, she whispers.

74

"People tell me that I like trees
better than people.

I say it's not people or trees.

What I like best are people
who like trees."

Selma James

WAGES FOR HOUSEWORK CAMPAIGN
London, England

A WORKING-CLASS GIRL IN BROOKLYN, NEW YORK, IN THE 1930S, Selma James was married at seventeen, a mother at eighteen. She supported the workers, but rejected the left-wing notion of manning the barricades and leaving home and family behind. How would the housework get done, she wondered, if the women wandered off?

Her husband, C.L.R. James, was a radical thinker and organizer from Trinidad who had been deported from the United States during the McCarthy era. With him she moved to the West Indies. Once again, she saw how crucial women's work was, how a woman would rise at dawn to get the housework done before leaving for the fields or the workplace to do her "other job."

Selma James

"*I remember walking into a woman's house and seeing children's clothing strung up on a line across the room. She said, 'I'm selling them. I need to make some money on my own.'*"

She was in her forties when she arrived in England, during the heat of the women's movement. She embraced the movement but did not view going out to work as liberation. She began then to develop her opposition to the trends — the double-duty women did, the upswing of the fight for abortion. "I thought that women wanted children," she says. "They just didn't have the money."

The movement, she thought, was very white-dominated. "I was not of the right, but I had a different perspective." She wanted to put women at the forefront of the struggle.

Her thinking solidified when a friend who had come from Italy asked her to describe this "feminism." "As I told her about it," she says, "I told myself as well." She realized that women were dominated by men, and dependent on them. "Our options are circumscribed by the reality of economics, and this economic reality is much clearer to women living on the edge," she says. "It is here where the end of a marriage leaves a woman with almost nothing."

Along with her friend, Mariarosa Dalla Costa, she wrote *The Power of Women and the Subversion of the*

Community, singling out housework, women's unpaid work, as the basis of women's powerlessness. It could become, she believed, their potential lever of power. From that book, in 1972, the Wages for Housework campaign was born.

She didn't stop there. Another book critiqued how the unions treated women, an attack that outraged the left. Then she wrote a pamphlet and in it listed six demands: one was wages for housework. Another was the right to have children, or not. "You must be able to see everything you do in the context of others' lives," she says.

Slowly the notion took hold, a realization that most of the work in the world is unwaged. "It was women who did all the work," she says, "all the work of the world that was not registered anywhere in the economic statistics." By the mid-1990s these statistics were staggering. World wide, for their unpaid labour, women's work was

valued at $11 trillion U.S. and the value of housework alone in the United States at $1,461 billion annually.

Selma James is in her early seventies now, small and slender, with cropped greying hair and expressive hands. She recounts the campaign's successes, through the 1980s, their work with the UN to get women's work counted, the growing recognition that women's work, wherever it is, is real work, exploding the myth that only if you go out to work are you liberated.

And they have presented this astounding news: that women do about two-thirds of the world's work for five percent of the income and ten percent of the assets. "That statistic," Selma says, "has made history."

Chatsumarn Kabilsingh

BUDDHIST ACTIVIST
Nakhonpathom, Thailand

BUDDHISM, CHATSUMARN KABILSINGH MAINTAINS, IS FREE FROM GENDER. It is the very first religion that considers women's spirituality equal to men's.

In the courtyard of the Home of Peace and Love, a temple that is a spiritual shelter for women, we are surrounded with Buddha. He is everywhere, Chatsumarn says, her eyes crinkling with happiness. The temple has pale green rooftops, scalloped layers of lotus leaves, carved relief in soft pink. Sculptures show women kneeling before Buddha and the entrance to the temple is marked by a large gold statue of the Laughing Buddha. Nearby, fat blossoms fall from the sala tree. Under such a tree, it is said, Buddha passed away. There, under the gnarled bodhi tree, Buddha became enlightened.

Chatsumarn Kabilsingh

Not so Buddhists in Thailand.

Ordination is highly valued here, but it is forbidden to women. There are four groups of Buddhists: monks, nuns, laymen and laywomen. Women have only a supporting role; in Thailand they may not even become nuns, sharing the shaved heads and saffron robes of the monks.

So what happens, says Chatsumarn, is that women think of themselves as lowly, as small and valueless. The society wants ordination for sons and in some families will ask their eldest daughters to pay. Sometimes the girls go to Bangkok and give themselves to prostitution.

People like me, she says, are always outcasts, peripheral. Education can change things, and Chatsumarn has tried. She is a professor of philosophy whose writings on Buddhism are read around the world. Spirituality is her lifeblood.

Feminists in Thailand are not using their strength, have fallen into the trap of believing that Buddhism is against women. Chatsumarn knows that this is not so. She has now taken the path of her own mother, has divorced her husband and travelled to

Taiwan to be ordained a Buddhist nun, as her mother has been since 1974, when Chatsumarn was ten.

Somehow, she always knew this would happen. She had rebelled against her mother when she was growing up, she says, against the expectation that she would become a nun. Then as Chatsumarn aged, the force inside to make a commitment grew stronger. "There are so many things in life to do," she says, "and time is limited. This is what I want to do most."

Chatsumarn will lead the Home of Peace and Love when her mother passes on, although the temple is not recognized by Thai Buddhists because it's run by women. But Chatsumarn has more important things to think about. While some people think once ordained you should remain quiet, she believes that to be Buddhist, you must be socially active.

Ordination is a secondary issue, she says. The primary concern is how people in this country can understand message of the Buddha. Then all problems will be solved.

"One time I was speaking to 200 young monks.

I said to them, 'You are an obstacle to me.'"

Olayinka
Koso-Thomas

ACTIVIST AGAINST FEMALE GENITAL MUTILATION
Sierra Leone & London, England

THE NATIVE DOCTOR SHARPENS HER KNIFE. WOMEN HOLD DOWN
a baby girl of about one year, who is crying, wailing, blood streaming from cuts across her face and
chest. These are tribal marks. The child's legs are spread and as she screams in pain, her body
writhing in agony, the woman cuts away the child's clitoris then her labia minor. Covered in blood,
weak with shock and pain, the little girl is given back to her mother. The women celebrate.

Many people believe in genital mutilation, says Olayinka Koso-Thomas.
So far, more than 120 million African women have been mutilated, twelve million on
average every year. It's done to a girl anywhere from her eighth day of life to eighteen years
and must be done before she gives birth because those who mutilate believe that if the
head of the baby touches the clitoris, that baby will die.

Olayinka
Koso-Thomas

Olayinka, who practises medicine

in Sierra Leone, knows all about mutilation, how it's carried out and why. It's the normal thing, she says. If a girl isn't circumcised, she won't get married. "The secret society, the Bunda society, they say, 'We're going to make you into a real woman.' They know that if a woman is not circumcised, she'll be a loose woman because the clitoris is the seat of enjoyment."

And enjoyment is not expected of African women. Marry and have children, Olayinka says; it's all done for the sake of the patriarchal society, to keep the women nearby, to decrease libido. Olayinka and her group, the Inter-African Committee (IAC) on Traditional Practices Affecting the Health of Women and Children, have been fighting since 1984 to have the governments in Burkina Faso, Ghana, Mali and Sudan declare the practice wrong. They believe it has almost completely disappeared from Nigeria.

It's the parents, she says, who must be convinced. "We show them educational material," she says. "We tell them that they don't do it in Saudi Arabia. I say, 'The prophet Mohammed did not do this to his daughters.'"

"A foreskin is bloodless, the clitoris and labia are highly vascular. If they did the equivalent to boys that they are doing to girls, they would cut off the penis."

86

But it's still done, over and over again, millions of times, often on festive occasions. The woman or girl is held down by other women and the clitoris and labia minor are removed, rarely with anesthetic. If they cut too deeply, they cut the clitoral artery. The wound heals with adhesion; in the Horn of Africa, where even the labia major is excised, it's held together with acacia thorns.

No one speaks of the pain, so the girls never know, she says. Their mothers or grandmothers take them; they're given liquid in the morning to numb the pain or in riverside villages in Sierra Leone they are taken to sit in the cold water from the waist down to numb their bodies. The female relatives lead the initiates into a hut and they all lie down, thirty and forty girls at one time. Then they are cut.

The mutilation doesn't stop there. Olayinka has seen the results of this procedure continue to mutilate and in some cases kill African women. "They can get urinary infection or it travels to the uterus and to the kidneys," she says. "Some can never have children. When you see the X-ray of a girl of eighteen or twenty who can't get pregnant, you see the uterus and the tubes all blocked from infection." The women also develop fistulas, when the scar won't yield during childbirth and the baby is caught in the vagina. There is so much pressure that the baby tears a hole out of which urine and feces will begin to pass. For her pain and agony, the woman is now considered unclean and is thrown out of the family.

It is because of these health complications that Olayinka and the IAC have been fighting the procedure, despite demonstrations and robberies at her practice in Sierra Leone. But even when she manages to convince a woman not to take her daughter to be circumcised, the mother-in-law or grandmother will entice the girl.

Education is the key, Olayinka believes. Educated people won't let their children be mutilated. "When a woman is suffering, and it could be years later, she rarely connects it with something that happened when she was eight," she says. Olayinka continues her work, even as she lives in exile in a London flat, and today there is a reduced percentage of girls being cut. But with millions mutilated every year, she and her supporters are a long way from winning their fight.

Käthe
Kollwitz

GUERRILLA GIRL
Culver City, California, U.S.A.

A WOMAN IN A GORILLA MASK MEETS US IN HER ALL-WHITE STUDIO.
She calls herself Käthe Kollwitz, but the real Kathë was born in the mid-nineteenth century,
a printmaker who worked on anti-war issues. This Kathë is one of the Guerrilla Girls, a group of
women artists whose campaigns, launched in the United States, are now held all over the world.

To remain anonymous, they don gorilla masks and
take the names of deceased women writers, artists and performers. "We're
masked adventurers," this Käthe says, "like the Lone Ranger and Wonder
Woman." The force of evil ranged against these masked women is
discrimination in culture, film, theatre, art.

Käthe Kollwitz

"It's actually great. You're yourself but not yourself. You're a symbol."

They speak out with their own art — more than one hundred posters, printed projects and actions. Their goal is to expose — using satire, research and their dynamic presence in gorilla masks — areas of sexism, racism and discrimination in the art world. With their books, posters and appearances at workshops and other public venues, they aim to embarrass the hell out of the powers that be.

The Girls started in 1985, as a response to an exhibition at the Museum of Modern Art in New York titled "An International Survey of Painting and Sculpture." It was supposed to be showing all the important contemporary art in the world, but of 169 artists, only thirteen were women and all were white, either from Europe or the United States.

Then the curator of the show was quoted as saying that any artist who wasn't in it should rethink "his" career, which raised a red flag for a group of women artists in New York. No way you would only find thirteen women, they figured, unless you were prejudiced.

Under the auspices of the Women's Caucus for Art, they demonstrated in front of the museum with the usual placards and picket line. But the women were mortified, Käthe says, by how ineffective it was. They decided there had to be a better way to break through the backlash.

The Guerrilla Girls were born. They went after galleries, artists, museums, critics and collectors, using a smart-ass approach and discovering that humour is an effective weapon. Their first two posters nailed U.S. galleries where ten percent or fewer of the artists were women. They started spinning out the numbers, presenting facts, shocking facts like the number of major American galleries that showed women artists in 1986. One.

Connecting all over the world through their website, they also started critiquing the art world in a much deeper way, charging museums with corrupt ethics, making this public with their creative use of information. They've gone after pop culture as well, shaking up the 2002 Academy Awards with a giant billboard in Hollywood showing the "anatomically correct" Oscar. "He's white and male," the billboard stated, "just like the guys who win!"

Today, gorilla-Käthe says, you're seeing changes in the visual arts, similar to the change in the literary arts that women writers have sought for decades. "I think we have contributed to changing the art world in that respect," she says. Granted, things are not great; it's really hard to make a living at art whatever your gender. But it's a lot harder to be taken seriously if you're female.

The Guerrilla Girls are having fun, exercising their creative juices, making a point. "Just a bunch of girls," Käthe says, "doing what we can."

Sharon Labchuk

ENVIRONMENTAL ACTIVIST
Breadalbane, Prince Edward Island, Canada

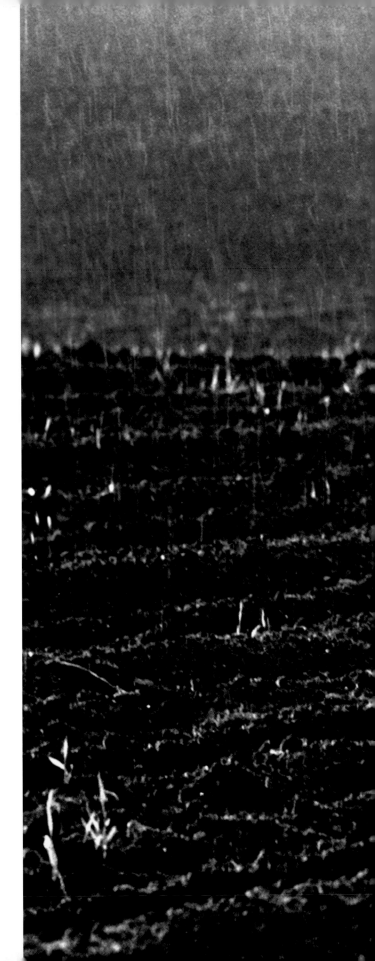

LIKE THE FICTIONAL HOBBIT IN J.R.R. TOLKIEN'S Middle Earth, Sharon Labchuk lives in a cozy house that is partially underground. The cathedral-ceilinged solar home, built with little money and borrowed expertise, needs nothing but sunshine and a cord of wood to keep the interior toasty warm during a Canadian winter. So who could fault her for enjoying the fruits of her labour, and the pastoral splendour of this tiny island?

But there's a poison wafting through her island paradise, and Sharon Labchuk won't be deterred until she has destroyed it, and transformed her home province into an organic garden. That is

92

far from being the case, so Sharon and the Earth Action group in which she is the agriculture expert are digging their heels into the ground and refusing to budge.

Because in Prince Edward Island, agriculture means potatoes and potatoes mean pesticides. Lots of them. Over the last two decades, Sharon says, there's been an eight hundred percent increase in pesticide use on the potato crop in the province. In 1999, for instance, more than two and a half million pounds of pesticide active ingredients were released into the P.E.I. atmosphere. "And this is happening when some countries have fifty percent reductions in the use of pesticides," she says.

At the same time, potato acreage on the Island has increased by eighty percent, meaning that potatoes are planted on one out of every twelve acres here. Potatoes are virtually the only crop being harvested from the fields of two-hundred-plus farms, basically an industrial farming operation to support giant, government-supported processing plants. One family, the Irvings, own and lease land as well as contracting growers to provide upwards of one billion pounds of potatoes a year, Sharon says. Despite the

subsidiary jobs created, she believes the cost of growing potatoes is just too high.

The entire operation is so heavily subsidized by the provincial government that she claims a real distillation of figures would show the industry could never stand on its own. But money is not the issue here. It's about pesticides, and the terrible damage being wrought in this beautiful maritime enclave known as the country's "garden province."

A garden it is not. Prince Edward Island has the highest hospital admission rate in Canada, and in the world, of people suffering from asthma. "The kids in schools here are all on puffers," Sharon says — those inhalers used by asthma sufferers when they have attacks. The province is also the site of an alarming number of fish kills, hundreds of fish that show up dead in waterways that border potato fields. A significant number of schools in the province also abut potato fields, and until now farmers have had the right to use pesticide spray right up to the edge of those fields — schools or no schools.

Not for long. The movement against pesticides is gaining mainstream support and the potato farmers are becoming very defensive, a welcome change from 1995 when Sharon first started trying to alert Islanders to the poison in their midst. Then, farmers were secure in their pesticide-using position, sure that most people found Sharon and her activist friends as nutty as they did.

Now, the provincial government is passing a crop-rotation act, demanding that potatoes be grown only once every three years on the same fields. And one group of citizens is petitioning its town council to create a one-kilometre non-pesticide buffer zone around it. No wonder: a dozen people were poisoned by pesticides in that very area a year earlier.

Even after the potatoes are ready for harvesting, the pesticide use doesn't stop. "The pesticide diquat, suspected of causing birth defects, is sprayed on the plants to kill down the tops," Sharon has written. "And finally, potatoes that are to be stored into winter are treated in the warehouse with a pesticide to inhibit sprouting. A P.E.I. potato, destined for someone's dinner, can undergo as many as twenty applications of pesticide."

Truth is, industrial agriculture can't exist without pesticides and chemical fertilizers, Sharon says. So why not take the 120,000 arable acreage on the Island and stop growing potatoes? She wants to follow the model used in Denmark, which implemented a 1999 plan to have only organic food supplied to all hospital and government buildings. A move like that would create incentives, and has a good chance of success given the small size of the Island.

"Until we make a commitment to move the entire Island to organic agriculture, pesticides are not going away," Sharon says. She's calling for the total economic transformation of the Island, an eradication of its poisonous ways. She wants it to become the garden it was meant to be.

"People identify with food growing. If you're not from the country, you don't realize how sinister it can be."

Emily
Lau

POLITICAL ACTIVIST

Hong Kong, China

SOMETIMES PEOPLE MUST PAY THE PRICE OF STICKING
to their ideals. Emily Lau says this matter-of-factly, politely, dressed in her
conservative suit, fine tapered fingers reaching to smooth strands of dark hair
behind her ears. She should know. Emily Lau sits in the belly of the beast.

An independent in the Hong Kong legislative

assembly, she is facing down the world's largest Communist government
while representing a community where people know little about
democracy but a lot about capitalism. She appreciates the irony of
her predicament.

97

In 1991, the British allowed elections for the first time on
this island where making money is the mark of success. But only eighteen
were democratically elected; the others were elected by limited franchise.
Lau was the only woman democratically voted into office.

She is not unused to the struggle to succeed. Her mother worked in
domestic service and it was her brother, himself financed through school
by an uncle, who paid for her education. She studied broadcast journalism
in Southern California and worked as a reporter for Hong Kong's leading
English-language newspaper and at Hong Kong TV. "I was diligent," she
says, her voice tinged with British inflection, "not a muckraking type."

Then she went to the London School of Economics to study international relations, working at the same time for BBC TV, when Britain and
China forged the future of Hong Kong. While there, she became indignant,
spoke out more. She successfully defended a Taiwanese girl who had run
out of money and she discovered the rewards of being assertive.

She came back to Hong Kong and was elected to political office for
the first time.

Now she wants to have a say in the future of Hong Kong. But this is a
place where for generations the elites were co-opted by prestigious
appointments, where the government used policy to channel people's
energy into economic development. The trade-off created a population for
whom money has more relevance than political freedom.

For Emily Lau, it's a pleasure to behave differently. "I just think that

life is too short," she says. "You've got to be able to do something you believe in." So she takes risks, as she did in December 1996, when the Chinese "selected" a chief executive and she and others protested and were picked up by police.

"I very seldom say, 'How come this happened?'" she says. "What I try to do is anticipate scenarios and decide if I can live with the worst case. At least then I can say that I walked in with my eyes open." Now she is banned from mainland China, like many of those who were democratically elected. She understands that her behaviour is, politically, not very ambitious.

With the current Chinese rule, the worst-case scenario would be crackdown, but she believes it's unlikely. People are afraid of the Communists, she says. So she continues to fight for democracy, for civil liberties such as the right to protest and associate, for political rights and the rights of women and children.

She doesn't hold out much hope that she will see democracy in her lifetime. "After all," she says, "a free and democratic Hong Kong would mean a free and democratic China." But one day, she feels, it will come. She continues to work, to be polite and diligent. Like any freedom fighter, she knows it takes struggle and time to reach a goal.

"My message is about **human beings having ideals and the** *courage to fight for those things."*

99

Joanna **Manning**

CATHOLIC ACTIVIST, WRITER

Toronto, Ontario

JUST AS SHE WEARS ECCLESIASTICAL COLOURS LIKE PURPLE AND red with flamboyance, sporting ruffles and patterns that proclaim her impact, Joanna Manning has taken the rigorous doctrine of the Catholic Church and set it spinning. She is a community worker, a religion teacher, has founded a shelter for refugees. Her home, a row house behind the city's bustling Kensington Market, is a bright and welcoming place.

A child in Britain during the Second World War, Joanna was influenced by the strong pull of resistance to tyranny and oppression and has always been, she says, looking for justice. But despite an early venture into the religious life, her search has led her on a collision course with one of the most powerful spiritual organizations in the world.

Joanna Manning

Maybe it was those childhood feelings about justice, or realizing that the saints had often stood out against the Catholic Church, but Joanna both embraced her religion and railed against it. She became a novitiate, but her early devotion to the traditions of the church gave way to questioning its contradictions. So difficult was she that the young nun was given exercises in humiliation — kissing the feet of her male superiors — to conform her will to the higher authority.

Attracted since her youth to the silence of spirituality, by the 1960s she realized that being a nun was not her calling. She couldn't stop questioning, didn't want to be celibate. She left the novitiate and began to study theology, the new theology of the Second Vatican Council. The Council, she says, brought out the call of the laity as the most important aspect of the church. "It was not to be a fortress. We were to be a pilgrim people in solidarity with the poor." Joanna had found her spiritual home.

She married and came to Canada, where her husband enrolled in the permanent diaconate program, designed for laymen. The wives began to read and discuss feminist theology and again Joanna began to speak out. Why, she asked, was I denied ordination because I am a woman?

Joanna was teaching a theology course for Catholic teachers-in-training when the crimes against the children at the Mount Cashel orphanage in Newfoundland became public. The abuses perpetrated by Christian Brothers on their students, the child abuse and pedophilia, were horrible. The silence and denial of the Catholic Church was deafening.

Along with a group of teachers, she sent letters to the bishops, arguing that celibacy and the authoritarian nature of the church had caused these men to regress to the point where they were operating at a pre-adolescent phase of development. They found women too threatening, so they sought out children.

Their overtures were rebuffed. And so they went to the media, with Joanna as spokesperson. She got letters from all over Canada, she says, from Catholics agreeing with them. Plus, of course, threats from the right wing. "But I also got phone calls from men in their twenties who had been abused. I had never dreamed people were capable of this, let alone priests. It was indescribable."

Joanna's marriage broke down and she went to Africa to visit a good friend, a priest. She ended up in a village in Cameroon working in a clinic, where most of those who came in were women who would talk about their problems. We love children, the women would say, but we don't want so many. The church, though, forbade the distribution of contraception. Their husbands, they told her, would go with other women or beat them if they tried to use the rhythm method.

Forbidding women any control over their bodies was, Joanna felt, another manifestation of how the church controlled the lives of the poor — in this case, the celibate male clergy ruling women's lives. She decided to act. "I thought, 'I'm not concerned about survival, these women are. They don't have time and skills to fight the church. I do.' "

Trying to give voice to poor Catholic women, she wrote a book, *Is the Pope Catholic?*, an exposé of the sexism within the Catholic Church. She felt she had to register her protest against the statelessness of women within the Church and, because of that, in the world.

She could see why this was not changing. Hadn't one of her own male students, when she tried to point out the injustice of harassment towards girls and women, replied: "But miss, you know that God is a man, that Jesus Christ was a man and women will never be priests. So you know women will never be equal." He understood, she realized, that domination was at the root of his maleness.

She is often castigated and criticized, but continues to bring the boldness of her voice to the discussion. "My message," she says, sitting in the third-floor eyrie where she writes, painted in dazzling shades of turquoise, blue and purple, "is that the ban on the ordination of women is contrary to the message of Christ. It cannot be supported theologically; it is one of the main causes of violence and discrimination everywhere."

"This Pope has shut down discussion on the ordination of women. But people in the world are moving towards inclusiveness. That's how we're going to survive."

Monica McWilliams

WOMEN'S COALITION
Belfast, Northern Ireland

FOR ONE KILOMETRE, A BROAD, LAMP-LIT AVENUE FOLLOWS THE ROLLING
Irish landscape until it reaches the doors of Stormont, the Northern Irish Parliament. Here a peace process and

finally a true government, the work of people with positions once fiercely held through the haze of sectarian violence,

is being laboriously, painstakingly forged. It is entirely plausible that none of this could have happened without a

coalition already in their midst, a political party created with the express purpose of bringing women's needs and

a woman's point of view to the process.

In 1996, University of Ulster lecturer Monica McWilliams and Avila Kilmurray, director of

the Northern Ireland Voluntary Trust, sat in a Belfast cafe and began to develop the notion that they could

bring women into political life. This was the moment when McWilliams and the indefatigable band of

women that became the Northern Ireland Women's Coalition took their first firm step on the long road that led to Stormont. To get elected, they pasted their candidates' pictures on cardboard boxes, covered them with cellophane and hung them with strings. They knocked on doors, boarded trains to hand out leaflets, gave speeches. Most importantly, they considered the issues, did their homework, presented their opinions.

Along the way, they have been called dykes, Sinn Féin in skirts, told they're in love with murderers. But they're non-sectarian, one of the few parties able to have good relations with both sides, and name-calling has not deterred them. Now, more than six years since the peace process started, they have fought six elections and two general elections, never straying from their path — to promote the principles of inclusion, equality and human rights.

Three years since the signing of the historic Good Friday Agreement, there are two members of the Coalition at Stormont. Out of 108 members of parliament, there are now fifteen women, three women ministers out of twelve. And while women are new to political life in Northern Ireland, they are no strangers to activism. About 300 women's groups and 3,000 community groups form the thriving civic life of the region. To bring their opinions to the table, the Women's Coalition urged the creation of a civic forum with sixty members, interacting directly with the Parliamentary Assembly.

It's been a long, slow process, but the business of implementing peace is harder than making it, Monica McWilliams says. The signs of conflict are everywhere in Belfast: the militaristic murals, the ensign colours on curbstones in East Belfast, the fortified entrance of the high court building. There are still horrific incidences of bigotry, murders, bomb threats. But she is passionate about the fact that the opportunity for peace has never been greater.

Look at what we're doing, she says. We've created symbols, like the new floral emblem, the flax flower, and the new name for the police force, replacing the controversial Royal Ulster Constabulary. People are talking to each other, the IRA have agreed to destroy weapons; the impetus for peace may have swept the hardliners off centre stage. When they arrived at Stormont, a building that in the past represented such discrimination, all 108 walked to a site by the side of that long road and planted trees.

Beyond the non-sectarianism that they espouse, Monica and her colleagues are also charged with raising issues of concern to women, like domestic violence and rape. When they went in, the Women's Coalition demanded family friendly policies, to the amazement of the men around them. Now they sit from 10 a.m to 6 p.m., in the evening only by permission of the Assembly. And they lobbied to have written into the agreement the rights of women to political equality.

Getting cross-community consensus for their policies has been tough, she concedes. But they would not be sidetracked from their mission. The Women's Coalition role, she says, is to create safe places, to find a way to make things work. They are there also as a message to young women, so lacking in confidence and uninterested in politics.

Her own interest in finding solutions grew after a childhood on the farm in Kilrea, County Derry. She was a student at Queen's University in 1974 when her young boyfriend, Michael Mallon, was tortured and killed by a Loyalist paramilitary group. He had been picked up while hitching a ride back to Belfast from Toome. Monica left Ireland, went to the United States, but couldn't settle there, she says. Returning to Ireland, she pursued an academic life, became head of the Centre for Research on Women at the University of Ulster, an expert on domestic violence.

There will be more elections ahead, and Monica McWilliams knows that the road to Stormont will always be long and costly. She feels that she has at least got people to think.

"Until now, our best and brightest have just shipped out," she says. "What I really want is to build a country where my kids want to stay."

"It's not the bloody end of the world if I don't get re-elected; I'd be much happier thinking I've moved something along."

Valentina
Melnikova

SOLDIERS' MOTHERS OF RUSSIA

Moscow, Russia

"PERSONALLY," SAYS VALENTINA MELNIKOVA, "I COULDN'T GIVE MY SONS TO the Soviet army." Her boys were small when Soviet troops entered Afghanistan and even then Valentina knew that to send young men into the army would destroy them. She had been around Russian soldiers when she was in Germany in 1975, had seen officers drunk and young conscripts beaten.

In 1989, Valentina's eldest son was eighteen, conscription age. So she found her way to a few small rooms in a nondescript building just around the corner from Russia's infamous KGB headquarters, not far from the Bolshoi Ballet. Along with hundreds of other women, mothers of students who were to be sent into the army, Valentina began her life of activism. Many of those parents, she says, had gone to see their sons in their army units. They realized that their boys were being mistreated, some beaten or worse.

Valentina Melnikova

"In the Russian army now," Valentina says, her eyes hard, "all crimes are possible." Soldiers can be starved, not treated if they're ill. They can be beaten and humiliated. They can be raped, even forced into prostitution. Any person in a military unit can be subjected to inhuman treatment, she says.

Since they formed in 1989, the Soldiers' Mothers have taken on the Russian government with surprising success. They have forced the early return of 180,000 students from the army so they can go back to their studies. The Russian parliament, the Duma, has adopted many of their legislative initiatives and, because of their efforts, the 500 conscientious objectors who refused to participate in the first Chechen war were not punished as criminals.

It was the Chechen war that made the Soldiers' Mothers a household name. With all the audacity and bravado of determined motherhood, they marched off into Chechnya to bring home the sons who were still alive, to find the missing and to bury their dead boys. More than twenty groups of Mothers went to Chechnya, and they defended the rights of their sons, whether they were wounded, captured or had decided not to fight.

Being in the army, Valentina says, is like living in a very poor house. Just one big room with iron beds, no bedding. And no food. In one case in the navy, the sailors had nothing to eat for one month. "They were like skeletons," she says. "Six persons died and the rest became invalids."

There are cases of soldiers who are forced to beg for money, on order

from the officers, and threatened with death. There is a military unit where officers use soldiers sexually; another where they sell conscripts into prostitution. Then there are the beatings: officers beat soldiers, officers beat each other, there is conflict between soldiers.

To counteract this treatment, the Mothers have consulted military experts, have helped write drafts of the law and organized demonstrations in many Russian cities against human rights violations in the army. They have assisted more than 7,000 deserters and their parents. The Mothers tell the soldiers who come to them with stories of beating and abuse that they should leave.

And while they have often been ignored or harassed by the government and the military, they have been congratulated by the Russian people and the international community. They won an international peace prize in 1995 and a nomination for the Nobel Prize in 1996.

Valentina knows their work is far from over. Each year, they receive more than 40,000 calls. Each day, scores of draftees come to their crowded offices and she sits down with mothers and sons, trying to find ways to get the young men out or to move them to a less dangerous unit.

Her hair is a bright red, a vibrant symbol in a gloomy world.

*"We want **a professional army**, where young men are **treated with respect.**"*

Robin Morgan

FEMINIST WRITER, ACTIVIST

Greenwich Village, New York, U.S.A.

SHE HAS PUBLISHED COUNTLESS BOOKS OF POETRY AND HER
classic anthology on feminism, *Sisterhood Is Powerful*, has remained in print for thirty years. But
for Robin Morgan, words are not enough. A political activist since her teens, she is one of the
founders of the modern American feminist movement, organizer of the 1968 demonstration
against the Miss America pageant. In 1984, she created Sisterhood Is Global, the first international
feminist think tank.

For her huge impact, Morgan is a small woman with a self-deprecating sense of humour.
At the back of the tiny ground-floor apartment in the heart of her beloved New York City, she takes
the summer air in her cloistered garden. This is not a simplistic revolution, she says. "More than
equal pay, I want to see a profound transformation of society."

There has been change, she admits.
Consider thirty years ago, when a woman couldn't get credit in her own name and date rape, marital rape and sexual harassment were all tolerated. Economically at least, there has been a paradigm shift in the United States — women entrepreneurs are the fastest growing group in the business sector. She is convinced, she says, that "global feminism is the politics of the twenty-first century."

That's the good side. On the other side, conservatives are still taking away women's rights, there is no economic parity, no control or even equal say in church and the media, no proportional representation in politics. Nevertheless, she sees women rising up and saying, "Just a fucking minute!"

Feminism, she argues, includes human rights, the environment and peace. War is a feminist issue since the majority of refugees are female. Poverty has a woman's face. Pollution takes its toll in cancers of reproduction.

In truth, since women are primary caregivers, there are no issues that aren't women's issues. Even aging, rural to urban migration, agribusiness that breaks up farms and drives families off the land — in all cases, we're talking about women's rights.

Morgan comes to her tough, uncompromising position from a place of comfort mixed with hard work. From a young age, she has been in the public eye, first as a child actor who was once named "the ideal American girl," and then as a writer and poet. She is an editor of the American feminist magazine, *Ms.*, and has travelled as a lecturer and journalist across much of the world. She has twice visited Palestinian refugee camps in Jordan, Lebanon, Egypt, the West Bank and Gaza.

The women's movement, in all its vastness and diversity, is using different strategies than it did thirty years ago, she says. It has become more sophisticated, less shrill. "Women are shrill," she notes with a shrug, "men are forceful."

The great force of globalization is a double-edged sword, providing information but proving itself beyond control while two-thirds of the world is illiterate, with acute needs. In different parts of this world, suffering and oppression differ in intensity and drama, she believes, but at the heart, it's the same.

"The reason a woman is starving to death in Rwanda," Robin Morgan says, "is intimately linked to women being forced off welfare in Spanish Harlem."

We must understand that all of the issues that affect women — violence, economic, sexual, nurturing — don't disappear. Taking control is a long, complex, never-ending process, she says, one that women are engaging in all over the world.

Speaking, she moves her graceful hands, one finger swathed in the silver coils of a Bedouin ring. Listening, she has encountered the stories of women time and again, repeated them at conferences and in her writing.

Poetry, she says, is a way of looking at and listening to the world. And when deep listening and respect are present, she rejoices in what she calls the "you, too" moment, when one woman admits to something and all the others nod in agreement.

Such an experience is dynamic in its power, discovered only if you don't assume anything and work hard. When it happens, and she has encountered it all over the world, it's gorgeous.

"I cast a wide net. I call myself a feminist because the word has an honourable tradition. But I'm more interested in what a woman is doing."

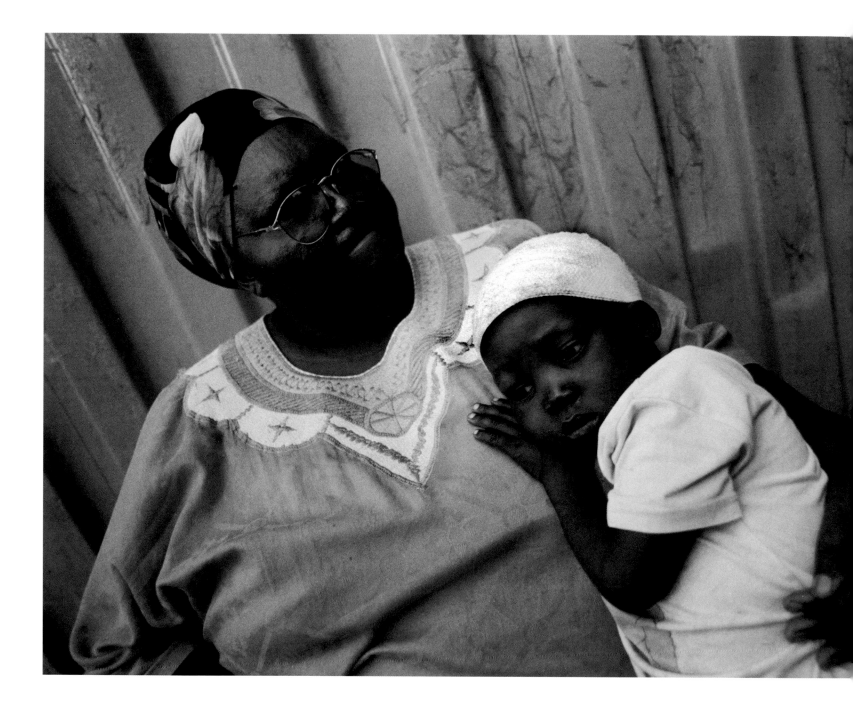

Zodwa Mqadi

AGAPE, ORPHANAGE FOR CHILDREN ABANDONED BY AIDS

Waterfall, South Africa

IN THE TINY OFFICE AT AGAPE, A HUGE STACK OF WRAPPED GIFTS FROM a local school wait for the children. It is just weeks before Christmas, and many of the fifty youngsters at the orphanage will observe this holiday accompanied by a deep loneliness that no gifts can assuage. Some are orphans, their parents dead of AIDS; others' parents are too ill with the disease to care for them.

Their greatest comfort comes in the form of a large, jolly woman named Zodwa Mqadi. She is the one who found the land, some few acres outside Durban, to house these children, and it is she who campaigns to find the money to feed them. "It's the right of every child," Zodwa says, "to have a home, to be loved, clothed and fed." She offers them these things, all the while trying to keep their link to their families, encouraging those who are able to take their children once a year.

Zodwa **Mqadi**

*"I hope to develop these children, **give them skills so they can stand on their own and pass what they've been given to others.** We say, 'don't look after your family only, look after all the children.'"*

Agape is meant to be a helping hand, but for many of these kids, it's so much more. Some are ill, cared for with the help of three volunteer doctors. Because Zodwa refuses to see a child stigmatized, each child is treated as if he or she is HIV positive. So when the children see blood, they are taught to run for help and never touch it. Many of the children don't have documents, but they are all sent to a local school.

Trained as a nurse, Zodwa spent years doing AIDS counselling. Then in 1995, she was invited to go to Uganda and there she saw the graves; seven from one family alone. "I knew," she says, "it was coming to South Africa." Twelve years ago, when she started working with HIV victims, the disease had struck one in every ten South Africans. Now a conservative estimate puts that at one in three.

At the workshops she held, Zodwa realized that people knew about AIDS, but nobody was taking note of the orphans. People would tell her about someone who had died and left three kids, or five kids. Zodwa confessed to a neighbour whose daughter she had counselled — the young woman had later succumbed to AIDS — of this burden laid upon her heart. The woman helped her get the place in Waterfall.

On this December afternoon, a group has brought treats from a local chicken restaurant. The children sit in groups in the hard-packed dirt yard, holding their bags of food, and before they eat, they sing. We are together, they sing. We are family. "We encourage them to sing," Zodwa says. "It helps in the healing."

The children sing, "God heals every disease." Their harmony impeccable, their voices strong and beautiful, they sing another song: "When you cross the River Jordan, you will be saved." The child who leads the singing is eleven; her name is Siwaphiwe. Her mother is dead and her father is now sick with AIDS. He can't be employed, he has no money, but still he comes to see her, Zodwa says.

Zodwa's granddaughter, Yilinasi, is also there. Just last year Zodwa lost her own daughter to an illness she's sure is AIDS. Yilinasi, just ten, at least did not suffer the fate of little Sifundo, five years old, who was found curled up inside a car tire. Without parents, he would wander around during the day and tuck himself into the tire every night to sleep.

The children, who range in age from one to fifteen, are sad and stressed when they come, Zodwa says. But after a while, they see the other children. They sleep in the main house, in bunks or on mattresses on the floor. They have pre-school classes in a huge container bin placed in the yard and play on a metal climbing apparatus. Now at play, they turn the balloons they were given into kites, and when one slips away there are quiet tears. Some of the children wear red T-shirts that say, "Abstinence Is Definitely Safe. AIDS."

Zodwa, in her large orange dress and kerchief, is surrounded by children wherever she sits. She calls a little one to her whose drink was taken, speaks quietly with him and wipes his tears. When the children arrive after school, they all come to greet her. They call her "gogo," which means granny in Zulu.

Children are abused so much, Zodwa says, not cared for as they should be. She wishes for every child to be brought up as a child, problem free, not worrying about where the next meal is coming from. "I would like to see South Africa looking after the children," she says, "as God would love us to do."

Priscilla Nangurai

SCHOOL HEADMISTRESS, ACTIVIST

Kajiado, Kenya

THE RIFT VALLEY IS ONE OF THE LARGEST PROVINCES IN KENYA, A VAST, OPEN landscape dotted with acacia trees where the Masai — a people known for their bravery and fierceness — wander as they have for centuries. Here, a girls' boarding school run by Priscilla Nangurai does more than provide an education in the primary grades. It is also a place of rescue for girls who have escaped arranged marriages, a permanent home to fifty girls who are outcasts and can never return to their villages.

Priscilla, mother of three and grandmother of two, is a Masai from a large family. She trained in the 1960s as a secondary-school teacher. After ten years of teaching, she reached a crossroads that was for her a lesson in pure discrimination. The school where she taught wanted to raise its standards and, in order to do that, decided to remove all its female students. "It really affected me," Priscilla says. She protested, but the girls were phased out anyway.

121

In 1981, she was offered a position at the A.I.C. Girls Primary Boarding School on the outskirts of the small town of Kajiado, which had been founded by missionaries in 1959. She quietly tried to understand why many of the girls weren't finishing school, or why their performance and attendance would inevitably lag. She discovered that girls would drop out because of pregnancy, often a result of the sexual activities that began around age twelve, after the girls had undergone genital circumcision.

Priscilla speaks out against circumcision — known by those who fight the ritual as female genital mutilation — but most of the girls cannot reject the cultural and peer pressures to go through with it. There is talk of ancestors, curses. There is also pressure to marry early. "Those girls who say no," she says, "are the ones who come here."

Her rescue efforts began in 1986 with a girl named Charity, who had gone home for the holidays and found out that her marriage had been arranged. She was thirteen years old. She sent Priscilla a panicked note: "I'm getting married," she wrote. "I don't want to get married; I want to finish my education. Help me."

The district commissioner got a note, too, and it was he who brought Charity back to the school. Priscilla was afraid of what might happen, but Charity refused to go home. "I always call her my eye-opener," Priscilla says with a smile.

At the school, a grouping of long, low buildings on eight acres of land, 650 girls board and study through the primary grades. Each year, between forty-five and sixty of them never leave. Others, even after they have entered high school, come back here to stay during their holidays; three girls at university still come to board. "My school is never too full," Priscilla says. "If a girl is brought, she will be kept."

With families, she always leaves doors open for discussion and reconciliation. The parents of all the girls at the school know they are helping the runaways and the parents of rescued girls are invited to reconcile with their daughters, although the girls are legally protected until age eighteen. Priscilla tries to show the parents that they will benefit if their daughters are educated.

This is the position she has also taken with the chiefs of the villages, many of whom have become strong advocates of education and have agreed, in writing, never to let the girls in their villages forfeit their schooling. They are often the ones who rescue the girls and bring them to the school. "We use the chiefs; they are very powerful," Priscilla says. "Now, whenever a girl enrolls in the school, she finishes. If someone doesn't return, we get them back."

On the windswept school grounds, a group of Masai girls come to greet us. They bow their heads so we can touch their foreheads, a Masai greeting of elders. Jedidah, now fifteen, came at age eleven. "My father wanted to give me away," she says. She told the chief and he came to rescue her. She wants to become a doctor. Sophia was exchanged for a patch of grass, Priscilla says, a piece of grazing land for her father's cattle. She was twelve. Mlenjo, a beautiful, shy girl with a smile like sunshine, is the youngest rescued girl Priscilla has ever had. She is nine years old.

Now girls are spreading the word in villages, talking to their peers, discussing their problems. "I can see we are succeeding," Priscilla says. "I'm proud to say that for the last five years, I've only lost two girls."

"*So many girls have been married off.* *I feel guilty; I see a woman and I think, 'I could have saved her.'*"

Tandaswa Ndita

MAGISTRATE, FEMINIST

Mount Frere, Eastern Cape Province, South Africa

SHE IS IMPRESSIVELY TALL — A ZULU QUEEN COMES TO
mind — and defies convention in every way. A mother of three, thirty-seven years old,
she is unmarried, wears high-heeled mules and dreadlocked hair. She is outspoken and
full of good cheer. And she is powerful, because she is the law in this region.

Tandaswa Ndita takes that power seriously, is infinitely patient in her
quest to gain trust and deliver good counsel. Born in the countryside, she received a
scholarship at age sixteen and studied law at the University of Transkei. She fell in love
with law, she says, with the way it empowers and liberates. She is one of four girls
brought up by a single mother — her father died when she was a baby — and the only
one who is not married. She graduated in 1985, and has been a magistrate since 1991.

124

In the countryside about an hour from Mount Frere, Tandaswa speaks to a woman sitting with two young girls outside her round Zulu home, while a pig roots and chickens peck in the dirt nearby. The woman, Rosina Nomalizo, tells Tandaswa that her three sons, unemployed, have gone away and so has the children's mother.

Riddled with arthritis, Rosina survives only on her government pension, and now she must care for her two granddaughters. In the home, the nine-year-old does the washing and cooking for the three of them. The little one is just four years old. They go to school, she says, but have no time for playing like other children.

As the women sit outside the hut and talk, Tandaswa makes Rosina giggle, complimenting the old woman on her youthful looks. But her message is serious. Women must stand up for their rights, Tandaswa tells her. "Things won't come on a tray, you must work for them."

She appeals to her to support the lady chief of the village and warns her, even though she feels protected in the community, to talk about any violence that may come to her or her grandchildren. The raping of

children must be talked about, Tandaswa says, and older women too are raped. "If you cannot stand together, you will become victims," she says.

She has seen many of those, especially the child victims of AIDS, the scourge of South Africa. Five or six children a day, two days a week, she says, are brought before her by grandparents who are left to care for them. To deny the problem of AIDS in a place like Mount Frere, full of poor and hopeless people, sickens her. "Any problem," she tells Rosina, "come and ask for me, the senior magistrate."

There are always problems, partly because there is a conflict around the law in South Africa — while the new constitution provides for equality clauses, it also recognizes customary law. Institutions promote equality, Tandaswa says, but customary law says that women are perpetual minors. So she explains their choices to the women, even though as a district court judge she cannot say which law should apply. "I am in hot ashes doing this," she says, her eyes crinkling with mischief, "but I ask them to choose."

Not as many hot ashes as in 1996, when the final constitution was drafted and she was part of the team, along with police, correctional services and social services, who informed men in the villages that women now had rights, even the right to refuse sex. Tandaswa laughs uproariously. "The men wanted to chase us out!"

Then there's the problem of customary rights, by which only male descendants have rights to succeed and administer the estate. But this statute was made in 1927 by the colonial government, and while custom should evolve and change with time, "colonialists made it difficult for customs to evolve," Tandaswa says, "and we are left with old ways butting up against the new."

To their credit, the chiefs have mixed feelings about all of this, she says. "They think we do have a serious problem, but if they don't recognize customary laws, then they don't recognize themselves!" Another great peal of laughter.

Now she is trying to help a local group start a shelter for women, some of whom come from many kilometres away. Tandaswa might issue a domestic violence order, but then what happens to the woman who must turn around and go back to her abusive husband? She just gets hit again. Tandaswa has experienced an abusive relationship; physical or mental abuse is just not acceptable, she says. A shelter would be a place a woman could stay for a while, away from the abuse.

She is the first woman magistrate in the region, a fitting role for a young woman who was always taught to be herself, never to conform to anyone's expectations. Her children, all girls, are nine, seven and six. Bringing them up, she says, is her greatest challenge.

"Sometimes changes have to be fostered; we can't always tread on eggshells. We should be equal. I know because my mother always told us, 'No one is better than you.'"

Chief Bisi
Ogunleye

COUNTRY WOMEN'S ASSOCIATION OF NIGERIA

Idoani, Nigeria

SHE WAS BORN BY THE ROADSIDE, WHERE HER MOTHER, WALKING WITH a calabash of palm oil on her head, went into labour. She is a chief through heredity, well educated because her father believed in learning and sent all of his ten children to school. These were the things she could not control. Then she began to forge her own destiny, always keeping her eye on that birth by the roadside, a child of rural Nigeria.

She is an economist, holds a masters degree in public and international affairs. But when charged with improving nutrition for the ministry of agriculture, she was perplexed by an unchanging pattern of need. One day, when she was visiting a village and expressed her concern, a woman said to her: "Don't be upset, my daughter. You say come here and we'll give help to the children. But you don't give us eggs and meat."

Chief Bisi
Ogunleye

So she decided to help the women plan their own destiny, and that is how her organization, the Country Women's Association of Nigeria, the first women's cooperative in that country, came to life. They started with 60 women; now membership exceeds 25,000.

She has spent time away from her country, has become educated, but Chief Bisi knows the way of the land. Her feet are rough and calloused, her features weathered by life. The farm women of Nigeria know where they're going, Chief Bisi says. They do eighty percent of the farm work and provide ninety percent of the food. They are traditionally the ones who train their children to save and spend. In agriculture, economics and development, they hold the country together.

But the women have no access to credit. They have no access to land, which belongs to husband, father or son. In fact, they don't own themselves; they are the property of their husbands.

How can a woman make choices if she is not empowered? How can she participate if she is not economically independent? "You have no money, but you have an idea," Chief Bisi says. "So what?"

The Country Women's Association started in 1982 with a radical plan to give credit to the poor. Chief Bisi implemented a revolving loan program, using her own salary for one month. If you are very poor, you get a loan three months after you have started saving. No saving, no membership. Before the end of its first twelve months, the Association gave money to fifty groups.

"The women were taught to make cakes. I thought, 'Why don't we teach them how to do more?' Everyone became tired of me."

After just five years, Chief Bisi says, a woman could have money, could eat three meals, put on shoes, live in a small shed, send her children to school.

She recalls how it began, her unswerving devotion to the women of Nigeria:

"I worked hard, like my mother. I married and we came to America, to Pittsburgh. I saw how good life was for American women. I thought, 'What is this?' This was going on in my head. I thought, 'Why can't I use the opportunity to do more?' I started talking about women in my country. I saw how little control they had. The more I feel bad, the more I believe something should be done.

"After ten years, we went back home. I went home to teach, but I wasn't happy. I wanted to change the system. No one was helping future Nigerian women.

"The government called for sharp graduate women to create a women's program. I was to talk about women and nutrition but I felt this eagerness to let people know, eagerness to reveal the secrets of these women, as custodians of natural wealth.

"The need to convey that was so deep in me. Cooperation, sharing, teamwork — these were the old ways. I know how to do it. I must find the language to explain it. This is my work, of advocacy, to form links to the people. All my life I believe in it."

Sebastiana
Pantó Pox

WEAVERS' CO-OPERATIVE
Chontalá, Guatemala

THE WOMEN OF CHONTALÁ ARE WEAVING. THEY SIT IN AN EARTHEN
courtyard, its wall of packed earth cut into the side of the valley, a blue plastic awning holding back the
afternoon sun. Thin bodies encircled by backstrap looms, their brown fingers move the shuttles back and
forth across strands of brightly coloured thread. Muttering chickens and doe-eyed children cross the dirt
yard, the smell of wood smoke drifts across the valley. Still, the women of Chontalá weave.

Sebastiana Pantó Pox sits among them, one of the first members of a cooperative
of sixteen widows called Ruth & Nohemi, whose weaving sustains families without husbands or
fathers. She is small and strong, with long dark hair and liquid eyes. Her hands are worn, her feet
encased in plastic slip-on shoes.

She wears the traditional wrap skirt and blouse.

Their elaborate motifs, heavily embroidered in bright greens, yellows and pinks, bring sunshine to this dark world. She weaves, as all the women do, to feed a family stricken by loss.

Sebastiana was a young wife, large with her second child, when the deadly conflict between army and rebels struck at the heart of her life in the valley of Chontalá early in the 1980s. Already, the soldiers had herded villagers into the pink stucco church high up in the valley and set fire to it. Already, helicopters had come with bombs, people were taken from their homes and killed.

The villagers were afraid, begged for mercy, for a way to keep their families alive. The soldiers felt in control. One day, they ordered the villagers to assemble at the school. They ran in panic to obey, but Sebastiana's husband, left behind in the cornfield, was surrounded and dragged away. She found him, hours later, thrown to the bottom of a latrine.

In the courtyard, the women are no longer weaving. The children become quiet, even the chickens stop rooting about. Sebastiana raises a small hand and wipes the tears from her tired eyes, remembering those last desperate moments when they pulled his body out of the pit, cleaned him with water, to find his face beaten, his neck cut. He died in her arms.

Now the killing has stopped. But what has been lost — the husbands who will never again work in the fields, watch their babies grow, love their wives — can never be found again. So Sebastiana looks after her family, tends the crops. The cornstalks rustle in the fields, the chickens strut about, sweet smoke lies across the valley.

Sebastiana and the women of Chontalá weave.

"My husband was surrounded by soldiers, his hands were tied behind his back. They were pushing him up the hill. I tried to follow, but they pushed me back. They told me, 'This is not your business.'"

Kim Pate

ADVOCATE FOR WOMEN IN PRISON
Kingston, Ontario, Canada

IN THE CELLBLOCK B RANGE OF THE PRISON FOR WOMEN IN KINGSTON, a prayer scribbled on the wall is a poignant reminder of the fragments of lives spent locked in these small rooms, each door a curtain of heavy steel bars.

Before they closed this prison, after years of lobbying and finally the revelation, on video, that women had been strip-searched and tortured by guards, hundreds of women were kept here, in two-by-three metre cells each with an open toilet and sink. Not only did these imprisoned women bear the torture of being locked up, they had to deal with the anguish of being separated from their families, for whom, in some cases, they were the only means of support.

136

Kim Pate has seen this close up. She is a lawyer and head of the Elizabeth Fry Society, an advocacy group for imprisoned women. She has an unyielding sense of purpose on their behalf.

It wasn't always like this. Coming from a working-class background, she believed that "you do the crime, you do the time." But after twenty years working with young people and sex offenders, and the last eleven years working with women, she no longer believes in prisons at all. Of the thousands in the prison population, she says, there are a couple of dozen men and a handful of women who are a risk for others.

Her thinking and accumulated knowledge, however, goes against the current grain. As the social, economic and political climate changes, Kim says, we're seeing more people likely to be treated as criminals. Why? Because we now have fewer resources to help people with mental and cognitive disabilities. With health care and social service cuts, people who were previously taken care of have been put into the community.

And now increased numbers of poor people, many of them women, are being charged with welfare fraud when the reality, she says, is that we have criminally low welfare rates. People can't survive on the kind of money in the system, so they try to find some way to augment that income. They're damned if they do, because whatever they earn will be deducted from the welfare cheque. And they're damned if they don't, because if they don't declare their earnings they could be charged with fraud.

We have constructed a society in which innocent citizens are seen as criminals, she says, when they attempt to survive. Because she has looking at the situation with a steady eye for many years, Kim knows how to solve this problem. Ensure adequate resources for people to live, she says, so that their needs are met. Simple.

What is more complex are the subtle tensions, the perception that certain types of people — usually identified as a "race other than white" — are a danger to others. These are the ones who are targeted, picked up, prosecuted and jailed more than other people. Look at aboriginal women, she says. They comprise approximately one percent of the Canadian population, yet they make up twenty-five percent of women prisoners serving two years or more and fifty per cent of women prisoners classified as maximum security.

There are three ways you can be classified a maximum-security offender, Kim explains. One way is to commit a violent offense; a second is to be a risk for escape. And the third way, the way that most women end up being classified this way, has to do with "institutional adjustment." Many of these women, especially the aboriginal women whose survival skills in prison are not good, don't adjust well to the prison environment. Women who have history of resisting colonialism, who have been used in the residential system, or the child welfare and juvenile systems, end up in the prison system, Kim says. They don't want to abide by the rules, so they resist. They resist, and they are punished further. It's also not surprising that women with disabilities can't adjust, so their institutional adjustment is classified as high. "One woman recently attempted suicide," Kim says, "so she was classified that way."

Given these trends, and the perception that Canada is soft on crime and soft on criminals, Kim's work with the Elizabeth Fry Society on behalf of women in prison is increasingly challenging. Although new, more "user-friendly" prisons have been built in the wake of the revelations of abuse at the Kingston Women's Prison, the reality is that the number of women in prison is going up and the resources to cope just do not exist. The situation for many imprisoned women, she says, is increasingly desperate.

"It's easier to do time than to be separated from your children."

Medha
Patkar

POVERTY AND ENVIRONMENTAL ACTIVIST
Narmada Valley, India

THE NARMADA RIVER IS INDIA'S LARGEST WEST-FLOWING RIVER, ORIGINATING in the state of Madhya Pradesh and winding its way through teak forests, broad valleys and fertile plains to meet the Arabian Sea some 1300 kilometres from its source. The basin of the Narmada is home to thousands of tribal communities and hundreds of thousands of villagers, and before that to ancient and prehistoric civilizations.

Into this valley in the early 1980s came the government of India, ready to execute long-discussed plans to create a series of dams that would provide, they told the people, irrigation and electricity. But their plans also called for a 200-kilometre-long submergence zone and the displacement of an estimated 320,000 villagers, whose homes and livelihood would be drowned under the waters of the reservoir.

141

In 1985, Medha Patkar also came to this valley. A community development worker, she walked from village to village along the Narmada, a slender young woman with a long, dark braid, talking to people whose lives, she knew, would change forever.

She wanted to know how they felt, how much they understood. People have a right to know, she thought; their consent matters. And what was happening in the Narmada Valley was not a people's plan. It had been pushed ahead by bankers and bureaucrats who had inflated the benefits and underestimated the costs.

She helped form a group called Narmada Bachao Andolan — Help Save the Narmada — and focused her assault on the Sardar Sarovar, the last dam in the series, close to the sea. It will cause an avalanche of displacement, she estimates. And after displacement, a bleak future. Of the more than 40,000 families uprooted by the building of the reservoir, only a small number have been given other habitation. Village communities have been dispersed, sometimes to dozens of different sites.

Medha spoke to the people, who understood how much she cared. As the group began collecting information about the project, they realized that many people who had already been displaced ended up without any land at all. Not only that, the electricity produced by some of the smaller dams had never reached the villages they were supposed to supply.

They staged protests, had to be forcibly removed from sites to be flooded, and went on hunger strikes. Between 1987 and 1990, Medha travelled to the United States, spoke in Washington and Tokyo, and convinced the moneylenders at the World Bank and in Japan to withdraw funding.

Fifteen years later, Medha Patkar's long, dark hair has turned grey. She has faced cheating and betrayals at every phase, she says, promises made by the government and never kept, court decisions that give all the power to industry.

She is well known in India, the diminutive, focused woman who has taken her protest from a drowning village in the Narmada Valley, as the rising waters loosened the folds of her sari, to rooms in Delhi where tribunals meet to decide the fate of the poor. She has never wavered in this fight for the people. Their greatest hope is to stop the dams within the valley; their smallest hope is for proper compensation, for rights to the reservoir fisheries.

Medha has spent her life in the conflict between resource communities and the industrialized world. She still believes, after all that has happened, that this struggle is something one can live for.

"It has always been the people who took the lead, mobilized by injustice. We activists are just the catalyst."

Lucilla Pizani Gonçalves

POVERTY ACTIVIST

São Paulo, Brazil

ON THE OUTSKIRTS OF SÃO PAULO, CITY OF EIGHTEEN MILLION, a home can be built in two days. This is how the poor claim land. They erect a cardboard house and then, eventually, re-assemble it in brick. The *favelas* rise along the hillsides, red brick homes, patched and jumbled. Some have been here for twenty years.

In a compound in Capaõ Redondo, at the edge of the *favelas*, Lucilla Pizani Gonçalves has dedicated herself to living out the theology of liberation. Since 1981, she has served the people of this community, many of whom come to learn about human rights, the law and leadership, to hold meetings or have parties.

145

Lucilla Pizani Gonçalves

In the low concrete building, where a wall of high windows faces the dusty drive and outbuildings of the compound, there is a large meeting room surrounded by offices and classrooms. Here, women and young people learn how to use the legal system to fight for their rights; leadership school has graduated more than 500 "leaders" into the community.

"God," Lucilla says, "is the one who comes to free his people from injustice and oppression." Lucilla, who is forty-one, has a close relationship with God; she spent eleven years as a nun before committing herself to activism among the poor. This is where she lives today, and she asks the poor, "Are you satisfied? What could make life better?" She works alongside them, offers encouragement, shares their laughter. She wants to set them on the path of hope and change, to give them the strength of solidarity.

Now, among the houses like boxes that edge dusty streets winding along the hillsides, there is a small park, a health centre. In the schoolroom near the church, children learn songs and letters. Everything here we had to fight for, Lucilla says. She wants the fight for peace to overcome the violence among the poor, the torpid silence that hangs over families even after a son or father is murdered.

This is a place where death squads are hired by shop owners to rid them of the young who rob and hassle them. It is a place where frustrated, hopeless men abuse their wives and police will kill and get away with it. A place where mothers have been heard to say it's good their son was killed, because when he was alive, the family was endangered by his enemies.

In the Cemetery of San Luís, Lucilla says, there are thirty people buried each day, mostly boys, half of them between fifteen and twenty-five.

The young have no work, she says, no way to change their lives. So they create gangs, or they write and perform music, singing songs that tell the stories of life here. The best-known song is called "Abandoned Place."

Lucilla knows that alone you can accomplish little, so she brings people together to fight for their rights, to fight for peace. The movement is growing, calling attention to the violence; the peace marches bring thousands into the streets. "All these things we've done," she says, "because of this struggle against violence."

"Some people think that it's okay to kill; then centres like this receive death threats and at such moments I am afraid. I'm very glad when I know people who fight for something, and when the room is full of people working."

Anastasia
Posadskaya-Vanderbeck

WOMEN'S RIGHTS ACTIVIST
Budapest, Hungary & New York, U.S.A.

ANASTASIA IS TALKING ABOUT HER CHILDHOOD IN MOSCOW.
She grew up in a family of women, poor but well educated, and remembers her mother worrying about her future when Anastasia confessed she wanted to study political economy and philosophy. "My mother was alone," Anastasia says, "so I knew I had to work."

She has surpassed her mother's expectations. With a PhD in economics from Moscow State University, Anastasia founded the Moscow Centre for Gender Studies at the Russian Academy of Sciences. Now she is director of the women's program in Eastern Europe for the international Soros Foundation. An intellectual powerhouse with fine blonde hair and cornflower blue eyes, she is well travelled, mother of a grown daughter. But below the surface of that accomplishment, there is a sadness.

149

Anastasia
Posadskaya-Vanderbeck

She was born five years after Stalin's death, to a young mother and an older man, a choral conductor her mother had fallen in love with. But Anastasia's father was excluded from an ordinary job or a place to live; his family had been the aristocracy, and in the Soviet Union that was reason enough to be cast out of society. "They lived in a communal apartment in one room," Anastasia says, "but finally my mother sent him away."

The little girl was cared for by her grandmother and grandfather while her mother, a chemist, went out to work. A professor friend of her mother's helped Anastasia get into university — at that time, without connections you were doomed — and she worked hard and began to learn about life. "I began to understand the difference between rhetoric and reality. But I didn't become cynical; I tried to be honest."

She was marked, also, by an incident when she was about eleven years old. After her father's death, she received a bundle of letters he had written to her. He wrote about the love he felt for her, his little girl. "I never blamed my mother," she says, eyes brimming with tears, "but I feel so sorry for him. I was his only daughter."

At university, she wrote about women and Marxism, about the demographics of women's employment in the United States. When she got to graduate school, she found a professor who would let her do a thesis on women. "I wanted to learn about Russian women," she says. "I was amazed there was so little interest."

By 1988, as the market economy was developing, she did research on women that showed social benefits could be lost. She wanted to warn people that without knowing the gender consequences of change, only the strongest would win. She became the first director of the Centre for Gender Studies.

"It was a very exciting time," Anastasia says, "to be at the centre of a new, independent women's movement with a voice that was separate from the state." The Centre helped accelerate the growth of women's groups, crisis centres, gender studies. She recognized the need to legitimize civil rights and women's groups while helping mainstream society to evolve.

Along with perestroika came many invitations to speak abroad, and now Anastasia has seen her own daughter graduate from university in the United

States. She heads the Network Women's Program of the Open Society Institute, part of the Soros Foundation, and spends much of her time travelling to oversee their work in Eastern Europe.

She thrills at the notion of bringing gender awareness into the educational, cultural and legal programs now in place. "Before 1997, there was no women's program," she says. "They said women were included but no one knew how, exactly. One of our programs is to review if women are equal participants here."

In the countries where she directs the programs, Anastasia will bring her educated appraisal to the political arena (where women are underrepresented), to employment (where sexual harassment is prevalent) and to the issue of violence. She cites these figures: a UNICEF report in September 1999 showed that 36,000 Russian women are beaten daily by their husbands; every fourth woman in Azerbaijan is beaten; in 1994, 14,500 Russian women were killed in domestic violence.

She's looking for more changes, especially when Eastern Bloc countries conform to the European Union regulations on gender awareness and equality, which they must do if they wish to join. Now, women's groups can actively use this as a tool, says Anastasia. Now is the time to be brave and bold.

"It's not we as women who have to adjust ourselves. **We want all of society to change.** *We want accountable, clear and reflected equality."*

Zainab Salbi

WOMEN FOR WOMEN

Sarajevo, Bosnia & Washington, D.C., U.S.A.

IN A GRAVEYARD ON A SARAJEVO HILLSIDE, THE FEELING OF GRIEF is palpable. Slender white columns with Arabic lettering dot the site; mourning families, here and there with a bunch of flowers, come to sit among the gravestones, inscribed during the 1990s, the decade of Sarajevo's greatest destruction. Those who lie here died in their prime because of it.

On a side street in Sarajevo, there is more evidence of the brutality of war. The large two-storey house here is a shelter for refugee women, many of them forced to flee their villages in the wake of ethnic cleansing. They come here, to a program called Women for Women, as a way of rebuilding their shattered lives.

152

In small groups, they get psychological counselling and job training, tools to bring them back into a world where they can think and work again. In the garden of this house, a half dozen women are making a sofa. One of them escaped from her town; her husband is missing and hasn't been found. She now lives in someone's weekend house with her daughters, who are fifteen, thirteen and ten. She likes to be here, she says, to be with the other women.

It was in 1993, with the trauma of death and destruction all around, the systematic rape and ethnic cleansing, that a program called Women for Women was launched by a young Iraqi woman half a world away. Zainab Salbi grew up in Baghdad, had lived through the gruelling Iran-Iraq war and had been in the U.S. during the Gulf War. She understood fear and hopelessness and, studying in the U.S., was horrified to learn that more than a million refugees of the Bosnian war were women and children, unable to return home.

Newly married, just graduated from college, Zainab visited the refugee camps in Croatia and there she met a woman named Aisa. "She had been released from a rape camp," Zainab says. "She had a husband and two kids and her life was devastated. We just cried and cried. After I met her I said, 'I can't go back to my normal life.'"

Coming back from the field, she realized that many people wanted to help. They just needed a way to do it. So with the help of a Washington church, Zainab launched a program to link women sponsors in North

America — who would each send a letter and twenty-five dollars each month — to women in Bosnia. Today, a woman from Bangladesh sponsors a woman from Bosnia; an American woman who got herself off welfare is another sponsor. Soon, the program was assisting thousands of women.

War is a sort of normalcy for me, says Zainab, whose slender frame and girlish good looks belie the harsh experiences of her life. "I grew up with the sounds of guns and shells."

And Zainab hasn't stopped. She has brought forward micro-credit, a renewals program to develop technical skills, a women's rights manual to teach through storytelling. Women for Women has distributed more than five million dollars in direct aid and loans in Bosnia, Rwanda, Kosovo, Nigeria, Bangladesh and, as of October 2002, Afghanistan. It is growing into a global network.

"You keep learning and see so much," Zainab says. "Now when I go to a country like Kosovo, I think about how people's lives could be better. I can see that it's possible to rebuild life. That's what keeps me going."

*"Everything can be taken from you in a second, **but the human spirit is so strong.** War can teach you so much about evil, and so much about good."*

Vandana
Shiva

BIO-ACTIVIST
Delhi, India

PATRIARCHY AND CAPITALISM, SAYS VANDANA SHIVA, ARE PART OF
one indivisible whole. All societies practising domination have had forms of patriarchy justified by
culture and religion. And capitalism? Well, the rush to exploit nature for wealth and profit has been
the reason for most environmental and human destruction. Patriarchy and capitalism, says the
physicist turned ecologist and activist, together have become the most dominant ideology of our
lives. The devastation created by these two forces could destroy us.

Vandana, a round-faced, full-bodied woman whose eyes shine with intelligence,
is not about to let that happen. She will use all her power to find the chinks in the
armour of this ideology and destroy it, piece by piece.

Vandana Shiva

Growing up, she was inspired by a climate of intellectual curiosity — her mother was an educator, her father in the military. That they decided to join the conservation movement and become farmers influenced her enormously. "I had no bias against small peasants," she says.

Vandana studied science, then she faced an environmental crisis in her region, and joined with other women to defend the trees. Their movement was called Chipko, meaning hug, because the women would hug the trees to protect them from being cut by the logging company. There is a point, Vandana says, at which you no longer make calculations about money. Then you plunge into what you feel is the imperative.

That imperative, she believes strongly, is solidarity. It will help reclaim the endangered spaces, will provide the groundwork to create structures that go beyond patriarchy and capitalism. Vandana's offices on Haus Khaz in New Delhi have become a mecca for those fighting for sustainable agriculture in India. There, in a series of small rooms on the second floor of a nondescript apartment building, visitors find the Research Foundation for Science, Technology and Natural Resource Policy and its director, Vandana Shiva, acclaimed physicist and now one of the world's leading bio-activists.

Vandana believes the process of globalization will destroy the natural world, and she stares defiantly in the face of this adversary, her weapons of science and humanity at the ready. In India, people use the streets, they fish in the waters and they harvest seeds for replanting. "We cannot," she says, "turn streets into private enclosures and farms into corporations, turn seeds into intellectual property, turn seas into a fisheries trade." If you do this, you are writing off at least three-quarters of humanity.

But this is what the corporations would do, with their seed patents, their takeover of the supply and marketing of medicinal plants, their attempts to convert the Third World into a consumer society. With corporate rule and unrestricted trade, you have a real assault on the livelihood of people. And you can't have a consumer society with poor people, she says; what you have instead is deprivation and famine. What will be sown, she says, is the greed of the corporations as they steal the last resources of the poor.

Now this huge, powerful system is confronted by two forces. First, the power of the ordinary people, who are being bound in solidarity, north and south. Vandana joins protestors all over the world when corporations and governments meet to plan their globalization strategy, and her Navdanya movement — saving native seeds to promote seed diversity — is growing throughout India. Second, and much bigger than the industrial machine, is the power of nature. The system can hide the financial chinks and flaws, but not the ecological ones created when genetically altered seeds contain poisons that kill life forms like bees and butterflies, or are rendered sterile so the farmer is forever indebted to the corporation for more.

People have been trapped into the idea of a higher standard of living, but now a revolution is taking place, one with people who see a better life means consideration of the environment and of each other. People, Vandana says, know why they don't want genetically altered foods. She will continue to batter those chinks in the armour of patriarchy and capitalism, and try to fabricate a green solution that will once again respect the diversity of the earth.

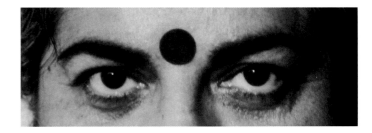

"You can be part of the ten percent and trample on everything, or you can decide to be part of that ninety percent. But **you can** *have a future only through more equitable sharing of resources and wealth."*

159

Siriporn Skrobanek

FOUNDATION FOR WOMEN
Bangkok, Thailand

MORE THAN ONE-QUARTER OF THE PROSTITUTES IN THAILAND ARE GIRLS OF thirteen or fourteen, says Siriporn Skrobanek. They are poor, uneducated and big business. She has been fighting for their rights for more than twenty years.

Siriporn has a quiet grace. Dressed in a tunic of raw silk with a scarf knotted about her throat, she acknowledges her own life of privilege. She has degrees from Thai universities and the Institute of Social Studies in The Hague, but since she was a student, Siriporn has been drawn to social issues, to help those who are oppressed. "I do this because I think that as a member of the human community you should contribute something to better the life of others," she says simply. In 1976, she formed a foundation for children; in 1989, she started a home for battered women; by 1992 she was in the thick of a most brutal and heartless business, the trafficking of women.

Siriporn Skrobanek

It starts with poverty and the urge for material things, sometimes just the need to eat. And now, with globalization, there is migration and poverty is increasing. Women, who are a large part of this migration, end up being used as chattel for prostitution.

Siriporn makes it clear she supports women's right to be prostitutes. Her fight is with those who hold women against their will. These are the trafficked women, ignored by a government that sees them as part of tourism, a major source of income, and then blames them by calling them illegal migrants. In Thailand, trafficking women for the purposes of prostitution, it is said, generates higher profits than illegal gambling, the drugs trade or arms trafficking.

Trafficking is a crime against women. Many women who choose to be prostitutes don't know they're going to be sold like bonded labourers, Siriporn says, in debt to their owners and kept locked in brothels or massage parlours. Often they are young, uneducated girls, brought in from the countryside with no idea how to escape or where to turn for help.

Trying to reach the young who are in the greatest

162

danger of exploitation, Siriporn wrote a book for children that tells the story of a girl named Kamla, whose rural family was so poor they sold her into prostitution. Unable to escape, kept in a locked room until she was wanted for sex, she set a fire and was burned alive. Kamla's story is true, she says.

So is the story of the twenty-three girls from villages in Burma who were promised domestic work in Bangkok but were imprisoned in a home and transported for sex to a massage parlour. They were rescued only when a customer with a conscience informed police. Siriporn was part of the rescue; her group helped the girls find work in Bangkok or return to their families in Burma.

Another gruesome truth: In the last five years, Japan has become a major receiving country for women from Thailand and the Philippines, who are swallowed into a system cultivated by Japanese criminal gangs and corrupt Thai officials. A few years ago, an estimated 100,000 Thai women were thought to be working illegally as prostitutes in Japan, where they become like slaves, Siriporn says.

"According to Japanese law, if you want to have contraceptives, you need a prescription. So these women have children who are stateless. Even to be deported from Japan, the women themselves must pay."

This is what globalization means to poor women, and it must be made more humane, she says. "We must examine its impact on labour and poverty."

Now, with lawyers and limited resources, Siriporn's group and others try to bring justice to women, to end their exploitation.

"The answer is *not to fight against migration or prostitution per se but* to stop the abusive practices against women who are trafficked."

Rosa Tarlovsky de Riosinblit and Berta Shubaroff

GRANDMOTHERS OF THE PLAZA DE MAYO

Buenos Aires, Argentina

SLOWLY, STEADILY, THE GRANDMOTHERS OF THE PLAZA DE MAYO HAVE BEEN knitting together the threads of documentation that might reveal the secrets of their loved ones' deaths and burials.

Rosa Tarlovsky de Riosinblit and Berta Shubaroff are part of this group. They have spent nearly thirty years sifting and searching, trying to make a recognizable whole of the torn shreds of their lives since Rosa's daughter and Berta's son, both in their twenties, were taken from their homes in the dead of night. Their children, they now know, were murdered by agents of the Argentine government during the "war against subversives."

165

Rosa Tarlovsky de Riosinblit and Berta Shubaroff

"We always had an idea of how it happened, but now thanks to testimony and the military people who confessed . . . Society knows the grandmothers were right."

It is their grandchildren, still in utero when their children were taken — born to mothers who were chained and blindfolded, then murdered — whom they seek.

Rosa is a frail woman, just eighty. She walks slowly, deliberately, but there is a set to her mouth and a steely look in her eyes. She is one of the leaders of the abuelas of the Plaza de Mayo, the grandmothers of May Square.

The grandmothers seek justice for their children, standing in protests in the Plaza de Mayo in front of the president's house, going to the World Court to advance their cause, bringing charges against the Argentine leaders under whose instruction 30,000 people "disappeared." They have also forced the government to recognize the genetic data that has been gathered to prove the lineage of their grandchildren, now grown.

They have located fifty-eight of the disappeared grandchildren so far, eight of whom had been murdered. It is part of the enduring sadness the grandmothers must bear that when their grandchildren are found today, they are the same age their children were when they were taken away — adults, no longer in need of a family home. The grandmothers must convince them, with all the patience and wisdom of their long years, to recognize and accept their legitimate family.

The tragedy that concentrated Rosa's life took place after the military junta took power in March 1976.

"In October 1978, my child, an advanced medical student and eight months pregnant, was sequestered. On two occasions, she called. The first time, she said she was fine but I didn't know if they had a pistol to her head. She called the second time and I talked to her and to a man who said the baby would be born, to wait for a call. The person said the charges against my daughter weren't grave and she would be able to leave soon. He said six months to a year.

"It was psychological torture to wait for the call that never happened. I waited and finally I realized things wouldn't happen that way. I started to work even harder after November 15, when I thought the baby would have been born. I looked in the maternity wards and hospitals to see if she had passed through. Then I went to the orphanages and nurseries and to work with human rights organizations already here. They advised me to join the abuelas. This was the end of 1978. Here I am still working.

"My daughter was opposed to the military dictatorship. They took her from her apartment with her husband and fifteen-month-old daughter. But they left the baby and today that girl, Marianna, works with us. Thanks to testimony of survivors, we know that my daughter gave birth, she had a normal birth, and she named her baby Rodolfo.

"At this time I won't make it easy on Argentina by saying, 'Yes, she's dead.' The state took her and the state has to answer for her. The state has to tell me: 'Who took her? Why? Who judged her? Who condemned her?'

"And they have to tell me where she is.

"I will never give up the hope of finding my grandson. As long as I have the ability, I will keep looking. I insist that young people have memory of this and never forget, because a country that forgets runs the risk that things will be repeated. My wish is that things that happened in Argentina in the 1970s never happen here or anywhere else ever again."

Nguyen
Thai Chau

CHILD WELFARE FOUNDATION
Ho Chi Minh City, Vietnam

ALL HER LIFE, THROUGH HER LONG SEASON FIGHTING FOR THE COMMUNIST party in Vietnam, Nguyen Thai Chau has taken the time to see the children. Born in Dong Nai Province in the south of Vietnam, she was twelve years old when her father was captured and killed by French soldiers. She was forced to leave school to help her mother raise her younger siblings.

Supported by relatives and a female teacher, she returned to school two years later and by the time she was seventeen had joined the student movement rallying against the South Vietnamese regime. She was arrested in 1961, tortured and jailed for three years, and was released into the arms of the revolution. She gave training courses for students, participated in youth and student workshops and always made sure to visit children in orphanages and shelters. By 1987, with the Communists in power, she was made head of the Committee for the Protection and Care of Children.

Nguyen Thai Chau

Now Nguyen Thai Chau, mother of one adult son, heads the Child Welfare Foundation of Ho Chi Minh City. The shelters she founded in 1988 — using a day of pay donated by her and by government employees — are safe havens for those she seeks to comfort.

They are street children: abandoned or runaways from broken homes, victims of sexual abuse and poverty, from eight to sixteen years of age. Found by police and volunteers, they are brought into the welcoming haven of the Green Bamboo Warm Shelter for Boys, or the Little Rose Warm Shelter for Girls, the first non-profit organization of its kind in Vietnam.

Madame Chau's roots in poverty, and her awareness of how the war broke families apart, fuel her desire to help. Poor children come from the countryside to Ho Chi Minh City to work and end up on the streets, she says. Or they come from drug-addicted families. Most girls come from families where there is sexual abuse by neighbours or relatives.

One girl was fatherless, living with a mother who was a street prostitute. When she was sixteen, a man approached her for sex and she ran away. She was wandering when she was found and brought to the shelter. She cried, Madame Chau says, because she wanted to go to school but was too old to be accepted. She goes to school now.

At the Little Rose Warm Shelter for Girls, Madame Chau is surrounded by girls who hug and hold her. Some are shy, reserved; others speak up, take her arm, wait for her caress. The shelter is simple: a courtyard that runs the length of the two-storey stucco building with a separate wing for girls who are ill or quarantined. A well in the corner of the yard is used for washing clothes.

When the girls come, they think their lives are broken, that they have been discarded. "To overcome that," she says, "we tell them that as members of Warm Shelter we give them responsibilities, like a family." The girls are taught to sew and each day they study English. They also get therapy amd vocational training, and learn how to dance and sing. They stay three to six months, sometimes up to two years.

Madame Chau realizes exactly how children who have broken families suffer without jobs or food. Looking about at the smiling faces in the courtyard, she knows it will be hard to change things when families struggle and society has little awareness of the rights of children. Through the care they offer, the Warm Shelters try to foster self-confidence. Now, hundreds of street children have gone back to their families; many come to visit the shelter during their holidays.

All we have to do, Madame Chau says, is long for a bright future.

"I come from a poor family and realize that I can help poor and disadvantaged children. In all my thinking, education is the best policy. This can give self-confidence."

Mama Toribia

NATIVE ELDER, HEALER
Ayacucho, Peru

SEVENTY-EIGHT FAMILIES CAME DOWN FROM THE
mountains into the Andean town of Ayacucho, driven there by war. Their leader
is Mama Toribia. She holds knowledge of the old ways, is revered as an elder
and wise woman.

As a child, her mother and father taught her how to
be in contact with the world. She never learned to read or write, but knew
how to communicate with others in Quechua, her native language. Her
parents advised her, gave her their wisdom. They showed her how to
transmit that wisdom, to live in peace with those around her.

172

In her mountain village, where the snow would fall in
winter and blot out the sky, she learned how to look after animals, run
a household and work in the fields. She learned how to see the future
in coca leaves.

Then in the 1980s, the war came. The guerrillas, in their furious
struggle for power, raided the village, burned the people's houses and
killed their animals. In a bitter irony, the rebels murdered her sister,
the military killed her father. Each blamed the other.

So Mama Toribia came down from the mountains, escaping through
the night with her own children and those of her dead sister.

She brought with her that wisdom of the past, using and sharing it to
keep the old ways alive. People come to her for advice and healing. Each
year, she asks Mother Earth for a good harvest. She is the midwife,
delivering babies, the healer who can cure people of negative energies.

She lives now on the rocky plain that rises on the outskirts of Ayacucho,
in a tin-roofed adobe house, one room with a sunken dirt floor and a bed.
In her garden, she grows corn and potatoes, washing is hung on a tree in the
terraced space that serves as kitchen and garden. She dyes her own cloth,
using for colour the cacti that grow in the high adobe walls. From the
garden seat, she can see the snow-capped Andes ringing the town.

Somewhere up there is the home she left behind.

For her people, Mama Toribia is the link with the past. She is history
and wisdom. Brimmed hat, shawl, layered skirts, dark eyes in a nut-brown

174

face, she carries the memories of their lives in that mountain village. They go back to plant and harvest crops, but no longer find comfort there.

"It is difficult to find the life again," she says. "We went back but didn't feel comfortable; the community was broken."

Their lives before the war is a story, treasured by Mama Toribia along with her healing ways.

"The Earth is like a mother that gives fertility. We call her Pachamama, a concept of time and eternity. I wish this wisdom might not be lost."

Jody Williams

LAND-MINES ACTIVIST
Alexandria, Virginia, U.S.A.

SHE'S KNOWN FOR HER BLUNT, STRAIGHTFORWARD APPROACH, SOMETHING
like the plainspoken speech ascribed to the Vermonters who are her kin. She has spent years on the frontlines
of activism - - in the 1980s with the Nicaragua-Honduras Education Project and the group Medical Aid for
El Salvador. In the 1990s, she joined Bobby Muller and his Vietnam Veterans of America Foundation, the
springboard for the International Campaign to Ban Landmines.

She pushed and prodded, spoke out at the United Nations, the European Parliament
and the Organization of African Unity. In five short years, the Campaign had joined others to raise
public awareness and Jody Williams was its most visible advocate, bringing enough governments
on side that a land-mine ban would be signed. She and the campaign were named co-recipients of
the Nobel Peace Prize in 1997.

Now the international spokesperson for the ICBL, Jody is no longer the one who gets up at 3:30 in the morning to send faxes all over the world, keeping the stream of information flowing so that groups within the coalition can assemble their facts and inform governments, build trust. Sentiment without action is irrelevant, she says.

But her work remains the same: sending out the message about damage wrought by land mines, about the need to destroy weaponry that has cost lives and disfigurement to civilians all over the world. People imagine that areas with land mines are somehow demarcated, like in the movies, she says. Nothing could be further from the truth. They put them along the banks of rivers, in the fields. Where people go.

So far, they have three-quarters of the world on board and more than 120 countries have ratified the agreement. Some have signed to look good, she says, others because of public pressure. They managed to get all of NATO, without the U.S., and Japan after receiving the Nobel Prize. She singles out Canada for its courageous position in taking a lead among governments. The United States, sadly, can't get around their military posturing, exacerbated now by the events of September 11. They are in the company of Iran and Iraq on this issue.

"My work is not about me," Jody says. "I only care about the message." And that message she will deliver with her typical straightforwardness to schoolchild, celebrity or prime minister.

"The land-mines campaign is a humanitarian effort and it's also about arms control.

The treaty wasn't the answer, it was the beginning."

Meilin Wu

HONG KONG WOMEN WORKERS ASSOCIATION
Kowloon, Hong Kong, China

BEFORE 1995, THERE WERE MORE THAN ONE MILLION WORKERS IN THE industrial sector of Hong Kong. Then China took over, and businesses started moving to the mainland, where there are few restrictions and even cheaper labour. Five hundred thousand people were laid off, most of them women.

As the factories were abandoned, their machinery packed up and carted away, Meilin Wu watched the Hong Kong Women Workers Association, which lobbies for employment rights for women workers, struggle to keep its membership. At first the group recruited in industrial areas, then they went into housing estates, talking to women, coaxing them to understand their rights with leaflets and street exhibitions.

Meilin
Wu

"In labour disputes, I would see how well organized the women were, how they had strategies.

I started to think more about why in their daily lives they don't have more opportunity to explore their power and ability.

I decided to work to develop that ability."

Those still employed face low wages, few benefits and age discrimination, in a country where it's hard to find work if you're over thirty.

Meilin knows what it's like on the factory floor. For seven years she worked in a metal watch factory in Hong Kong, counting herself lucky that, unlike her sisters who started working at eleven and twelve to support the family, she was able to finish school before finding work. It was during this time that she became involved in social action, first as a volunteer, then working for a labour organization, handling small labour disputes.

She studied labour law, tried to analyze the social problems. The growing unemployment is described by the government as "structural," and since there is no support for factory workers, the Association works on issues like unemployment benefits. Many women workers here are simply described as housewives, she says.

This is a typical scenario: A woman cleaner, an immigrant from China who has been here for three years, earns $3,800 H.K. ($487 U.S.) per month for working nine hours a day, six days a week. If she gets sick, she will get no wages because the labour law allows paid sick leave only if you're still away after four days, and only for workers who bring a doctor's certificate. As the sole income earner in her home, this woman cannot afford to be unpaid for even one day. She cannot afford to be sick.

The Association was founded in 1989 when a group of social workers, labour organizers and grassroots women workers got together to fight a proposal that would have cut off welfare to pregnant women. They discovered during this campaign that the men weren't concerned about protecting women workers. Meilin began to see that she needed to really understand the situation facing women. She is now coordinator of the Association.

The most serious problem is unemployment, she says, as she wanders by the doorways of empty factories and silent alleys where once the clatter of industry sounded. The government says it's the women's problem.

So the women are trying to solve the problem, to empower their membership by bringing women together to exchange ideas and learn. This way, they gain confidence and are less demoralized when job seeking. But Meilin knows that while the cooperative experience can give strength, it can't give employment.

Acknowledgements

Womankind was made possible with the generous support of the following:

The Canada Council for the Arts, Millennium Fund • Bank of Montreal • Air Canada • KLM-Northwest Airlines • Y.W.C.A., Canada • Toronto Black and White, Canada • John and Lettie Carter, USA • Ms. Nancy Ruth, Canada • Ms. Joan Lindley, USA • Nikon Canada • Pam and Red Ackerman, Canada

Thank you: Maria Peluso in Montreal, Canada, for all her support and wisdom. John Mahoney and Dave Sidaway in Canada, for their expertise and support in editing the photography. Wordsmith Mark Abley in Montreal for his superior editing skills. Johanne Totta and Gemma Raeburn, for their faith in us. From Nance to Steve and Carrie, for always being there for the kids; to my sisters, mother and father for always being there for me; to Hannah and Joe, for saying "yes" whenever I called collect and for putting up with their travel-weary mother. Patrick Redgrave, for being our international banker and general emergency man. Thank you for your limitless wisdom, patience and love. From Donna to Marc and the kids for thriving while I travelled; and to my folks for bailing me out in Nairobi. Susan Sansome and John Wallace in London for Notting Hill and more; Anne Tremblay in Paris for an office to nap in; Anita Borg in California, for cooking a lovely dinner. Adelia Liverani for believing in our project. Jackie and Walter at the Ruth & Nohemi Cooperative in Guatemala, UPAVIM in Guatemala City and Tarcila Rivera Zea of CHIRIPAQ in Lima, Peru. The guys at EOS in Lima Peru; Ronny at Enlaces, Internet Café in Antigua, Guatemala; the staff at the Swiss Hotel in Bangkok; Monica in São Paulo. Enakshi Thukral in Dehli, India, for sharing her friends and family. Karnail in Delhi, India, for his cab driving and bartering services. The wonderful stewardess on the Air Canada flight from Vancouver to Hong Kong. Jeanie and Charlie Shriver for the wonderful stay in Palos Verdes, California; Shiphrah at FAWE in Nairobi, Kenya; Randi Ewing for her translation skills with the Grandmothers of the Plaza de Mayo; Langa Dubé and Emmanuel, and for her amazing picnics, Ann Starkey at Dolphin Beach Villa in Durban, South Africa. Andrée Lauzon, for her elegant design sense. And to all the women who have taken the time and energy to share their stories.

Notes on the Photographs

iv Peruvian elder Mama Toribia at her home in the Andean town of Ayacucho, 1999; viii Veiled women walking through the town of Shapur Jat, India, 2000; 4 Anisia Achieng photographed in the offices of the Sudanese Women's Voice for Peace, Nairobi, Kenya. December 2001; 8 Georgina Ashworth in her back yard in Chiddingfold, England. December 2001; 12 Angela Bailōn Pérez photographed on the rooftop of UPAVIM in La Esperanza, a slum district on the outskirts of Guatemala City. November 1999; 16 Emma Bonino sits in the square of the Pantheon in Rome, Italy. October 2000; 20 Anita Borg photographed in her home in Palo Alto, California. March 2000; 24 Dr. Helen Caldicott on the parched earth in a Plattsburg, N.Y. vacant lot. September 2001; 28 Nancy Cardia in the museum that once housed police torture cells. São Paulo, Brasil. December 1999; 32 Clementina Chery, in her home in Dorchester, Massachsetts, U.S.A. September 2000; 36 Katsi Cook, photographed on her farm near Ithaca, New York, U.S.A. August 2000; 40 Ágnes Daróczi (right) and her mother share a joke outside their family home. Budapest, Hungary. October 2000; 44 Françoise David sits on a roadway near Ste-Marthe, Quebec, Canada. August 2000; 48 Leslie deBeauvais with a mask made by a rape victim. North Hollywood, California, U.S.A. November 2000; 52 Nawal el Saadawi photographed near an airport hotel as she prepares to leave Miami, Florida, U.S.A. November 1999; 56 Tahmeena Faryal conceals her identity in a university hallway. Toronto, Canada. June 2000; 60 Jane Frost and Brenda Hochachka at the water's edge at Spanish Banks. Vancouver, British Columbia, Canada. February 2000; 64 Street children cling to the hands of Enakshi Ganguly Thukral. Delhi, India. March 2000; 68 Nathalie Geismar Bonnemains with daughter Nathalie outside the fences of a nuclear waste plant. Cherbourg, France. October 2000; 72 Adriana Hoffman photographed in her forest, Mapulemu, above Santiago, Chile. December 1999; 76 Selma James stands behind a clothesline in an alley near the Crossroads Women's Centre, London, England. October 2000; 80 Chatsumarn Kabilsingh in the Temple of the Laughing Bhudda, outside Bangkok, Thailand. February 2000; 84 Olayinka Koso-Thomas photographed in her flat in London, England. October 2000; 88 Guerilla Girl, Käthe Kollwitz, near her studio, Culver City, California. December 2000; 92 Sharon Labchuk sits in a farmer's field in a downpour. Victoria, P.E.I., Canada. August 1998; 96 Emily Lau on the rooftop of the Legislative Assembly building. Hong Kong, China. February 2000; 100 Joanna Manning photographed in her home. Toronto, Ontario. November 2000; 104 Monica McWilliams stands on the road leading to Stormont, the Northern Irish parliament. Belfast, Northern Ireland. December 2001; 108 Valentina Melmikov in front of the offices of Soldiers' Mothers in Moscow, Russia. October 2000; 112 Robin Morgan in her Greewich Village garden. New York City, U.S.A. September 2000; 116 Zodwa Mqadi photographed with one of the smallest orphans at the AGAPE orphanage. Waterfall, South Africa. December 2001; 120 Priscilla Nangurai with Masai students Priscilla and Sophia at the A.I.C. Girls Primary Boarding School in the Rift Valley, Kajiado, Kenya. December 2001; 124 Tandaswa Ndita laughs with a Bhaca woman and her grandchildren. Ngwetsheni, South Africa. December 2001; 128 Chief Bisi Ogunleye, photographed in New York City, New York, U.S.A., while attending a WEDO conference. September 2000; 132 Sebastiana Pantó Pox stands with two other weavers in the countryside near Chontala, Guatemala. December 1999; 136 Kim Pate with her little daughter, Madison, in the Kingston Women's Prison. Kingston, Ontario, Canada. August 2000; 140 Medha Patkar photographed in the wetlands surrounding Delhi, India. March 2000; 144 Lucilla Pizani Gonçalves hugs a friend in the favela outside São Paulo, Brasil. December 1999; 148 Anastasia Posadskaya-Vanderbeck stands in the doorway of the Soros Foundation offices. Budapest, Hungary. October 2000; 152 Zainab Salbi photographed in a studio near Picadilly Circus. London, England. October 2000; 156 Dr. Vandana Shiva at her offices in New Delhi, India. March 2000; 160 Siriporn Skrobanek opens the window to the Foundation for Women, Bangkok, Thailand. February 2000; 164 Berta Shubaroff and Rosa Tarlovsky de Riosinblit outside the Grandmothers of the Plaza de Mayo offices. Buenos Aires, Argentina. December 1999; 168 Nguyen Thai Chau with some of the residents of the Little Rose Warm Shelter for Girls. Ho Chi Min City, Vietnam. February 2000; 172 Mama Toribia through the gates of her home on the outskirts of Ayacucho, Peru. December 2000; 176 Jody Williams reads through briefs at her home office in Alexandria, Virginia, U.SA. September 2000; 180 Meilin Wu in an alley behind factories in the textile district of Kowloon, Hong Kong, China. February 2000; 184 Guatemalan women walking with laundry, Santiago, Guatemala, 1999.

186

Further Reading

Georgina Ashworth

Gendered Governance – An Agenda for Change. UNDP, 1996.

Changing the Discourse: A Guide to Women's Human Rights. CHANGE, 1993.

A Diplomacy of the Oppressed, New Directions in International Feminism. Editor. Zed Books, 1993.

Helen Calidcott

The New Nuclear Danger: George Bush's Military Industrial Complex. The New Press in the U.S.; Scribe Publishing in Australia, 2002

Nuclear Madness: What You Can Do. New York, Norton and Company, 1994.

If you Love this Planet: A Plan to Heal the Earth. New York, Norton and Company, 1992.

Missile Envy: The Arms Race and Nuclear War (revised edition). New York, Bantam Books, 1986.

Nancy Cardia

"Urban Violence in São Paulo." Woodrow Wilson International Center for Scholars, Washington D.C., 2000.

Nawal el Saadawi

A Daughter of Isis: The Autobiography of Nawal El Saadawi. Translated By Sherif Hetata. New York: St. Martins Press, 1999.

North/South: The Nawal El Saadawi Reader. (A collection of essays, conference papers, article and book excerpts.) Zed Press, 1997.

Memoirs from the Women's Prison. (Mudhakkirat fi Sijn al-Nisa, 1984) Translated by Marilyn Booth. University of California, 1994.

She Has No Place in Paradise. (Kanat Hiya al-Ad'af, 1979) Translated by Shirley Eber, Methuen, 1989.

The Fall of the Imam (Suqut al-Imam, Dar al-Mustaqbal al-'Arabi, 1987.) Translated by Sherif Hetata, Methuen, 1988.

Two Women in One (Imra'tani fi-Imra'a, 1983) Translated by Osman Nusairi and Jana Gough, Al- Saqi, 1985, Seal, 1986.

Woman at Point Zero, Zed Press, previously published as Imra'a 'ind Nuqtat al-Sifr. Beirut: Dar al Adab, 1979.

Guerrilla Girls

The Guerrilla Girls' Bedside Companion to the History of Western Art, 1998.

Selma James

The Global Kitchen: The Case for Counting Unwaged Work. Editor. Crossroads, 1995.

The Ladies and the Mammies: Jane Austen and Jean Rhys. Falling Wall Press, 1983.

Sex, Race and Class. Bristol: Falling Wall, 1975.

The Power of Women and the Subversion of the Community. With Mariarosa Dalla Costa. Falling Wall Press, 1975, 1972.

Chatsumarn Kabilsingh

Thai Women in Buddhism. Parallax Press, 1991.

Olayinka Koso-Thomas

Female Circumcision: A Strategy for Eradication. Zed Books, London, 1987.

Emily Lau
The Good Society: Is Near Enough Good Enough? 1997.

Joanna Manning
Take Back the Truth: Confronting the Papal Power and the Religious Right. Crossroads, 2002.
Is the Pope Catholic? A Woman Confronts her Church. Malcolm Lester Books, 1999; Raincoast Books, 2002.

Monica McWilliams
Taking Domestic Violence Seriously: Issues for the Criminal Justice System. HMSO, 1996.
Bringing It Out in the Open: Domestic Violence in Northern Ireland. HMSO, 1993.

Robin Morgan
Saturday's Child: A Memoir. Norton, 2000.
The Anatomy of Freedom. Norton, 1994.
The Demon Lover: The Roots of Terrorism. Norton, 1989 and Washington Square Press, 2001.
Sisterhood Is Global. Doubleday/Anchor, 1984; Feminist Press edition 1996.
Sisterhood Is Powerful. Random House/Vintage, 1970.

Anastasia Posadskya-Vanderbeck
A Revolution of Their Own. Editor, with Barbara Alpern Engel. Westview Press, 1998.

Revolutionary Association of Women of Afghanistan
RAWA in the World Media. RAWA, 2002.

Vandana Shiva
Water Wars: Privatization, Pollution, and Profit. South End Press, 2002.
Stolen Harvest: The Hijacking of the Global Food Supply. South End Press, 1999.
Biopiracy: The Plunder of Nature and Knowledge. South End Press, 1997.
The Violence of the Green Revolution: Third World Agriculture, Ecology and Politics. Zed Books, 1992.
Staying Alive: Women, Ecology and Development. Zed Books, 1989.

Siriporn Skrobanek
The Traffic in Women: Human Realities of the International Sex Trade, with Nattaya Boonpakdee and Chutima Jantateero. Foundation for Women, 1997.

Enakshi Ganguly Thukral
Big Dams, Displaced People: Rivers of Sorrow, Rivers of Change. Editor. Sage Publications, 1992.

Jody Williams
The Art of Peace: Nobel Laureates Discuss Human Rights, Conflict and Reconciliation. Edited by Jeffrey Hopkins. Snow Lion Publications, 2000

About the Women

Anisia K. Achieng heads the Sudanese Women's Voice for Peace.
Sudanese Women's Voice for Peace
P.O. Box 10737
00100 (GPO)
Nairobi, Kenya
Tel: 254-2-446045
Fax: 254-2-44-498

Georgina Ashworth is the founder of CHANGE, one of the first woman's rights NGOs in the world, with offices in Chiddingfold, Surrey, England.
Tel.: +44 (0) 207 733 6525
Fax: +44 (0) 207 733 9923
E-mail: change@sister.com

Emma Bonino has been elected for her fifth term as a Member of the European Parliament. She sits on the Committee on Foreign Affairs, Human Rights, Common Security and Defence Policy, and is a member of the Committee on Development and Cooperation, and the Substitute Delegation for relations with the Mashreq countries and the Gulf.
Web site: www.radicalparty.org

Natalie Geismar Bonnemains is a founding member of Le Collectif des Mères en Colère (Angry Mothers' Collective).
50840 Fermanville, France.
Tel: +33-23344-5251; Fax: +33-23344-1615

Anita Borg is the Founder and CEO of the Institute for Women and Technology. In 2002 she was recognized with the Heinz Award for Technology, the Economy and Employment.

Institute for Women and Technology
1501 Page Mill Road,
ms 1105, Palo Alto, CA 94304.
Web site: www.iwt.org

For decades, Dr. Helen Caldicott has been fighting the nuclear arms buildup. She is the subject of the National Film Board of Canada feature, "If You Love This Planet." Her home base is Victoria, Australia.
Web site: www.noradiation.org/caldicott
E-mail: hcaldic@cci.net.au

Nancy Cardia is Research Coordinator, Center for the Study of Violence, at the University of Sao Paulo, Brazil.

Nguyen Thai Chau is executive director of the Ho Chi Minh City Child Welfare Foundation.
Ho Chi Minh City Child Welfare Foundation
18 Pham Viuet Chanh, Q. Binh Thanh, TP.
Ho Chi Minh City
Tel: (84.8) 8.401.406
Fax: (84.8) 8.401.407
E-mail: hcwf@htco.com.vn

Clementina Chery and her husband Joseph founded The Louis D. Brown Peace Institute in 1994 to continue the peacemaking legacy of their late son, Louis D. Brown.
Louis D. Brown Peace Institute
5 Louis D. Brown Way
Dorchester, MA, 02124-1011
Tel: 617-825-1917
Fax: 617-265-2278
Web site: www.institute4peace.org/institute.html

Katsi Cook, of the wolf clan, is a mother of five children and grandmother of two. She makes her home at Crow's Hill Farm in New York state. Katsi is Director/Field Coordinator of the lewirokwas (Pulling the Baby Out of the Earth) Program of Running Strong for American Indian Youth. She is also a Midwifery Instructor at the Six Nations Birthing Centre in Grand River, Ontario, and author of "Berry Plants for Women's Nutrition and Medicine" In Vol. 1, No. 4 of *Indigenous Woman*.
Web site: www.nativemidwifery.com/katsibio.html

Ágnes Daróczi is a Romany activist who founded the Romedia Foundation in Hungary. Romedia Foundation: Pozsonyi u. 44, 1133 Budapest
E-mail: batsonyj@mail.matav.hu

Françoise David, a social activist living in Montreal, Canada, is a founder of the World March for Women.

Leslie deBeauvais is executive director of the Theatre of Hope for Abused Women.
11050 Magnolia Blvd.
NOHO Arts District
North Hollywood, CA, 91601
Tel: (818) 766-9702
Web site: www.hollywoodregistry.com/thaw3.htm

Nawal el Saadawi is a teacher and activist for the rights of Muslim women. She lives in Cairo, Egypt. Her autobiography, *A Daughter of Isis*, was published in 1999. She is a member of the Sisterhood Is Global Institute.

Tahmeena Faryal, once known as Treena, is a member of the Revolutionary Association of Women of Afghanistan or RAWA.
RAWA
P.O.Box 374
Quetta, Pakistan
Tel: 0092-300-8551638
Fax: 001-760-2819855 (USA)
0044-870-1394051 (UK)
Web site: www.rawa.org

Jane Frost and Brenda Hochachka are members of the Vancouver Dragonboat team, Abreast in a Boat.
Abreast In A Boat Society
109-1279 Nicola Street
Vancouver, B.C. Canada
V6G 2E8
Web site: www.abreastinaboat.com

Lucilla Pizani Gonçalves is co-ordinator at the Centre for Human Rights in Sao Paolo, Brazil.
E-mail: cdhep@uol.com.br

Adriana Hoffmann is an environmental activist and the founder of Defenders of the Chilean Forests (Defensores del Bosque Chileno). She is now executive director of Conama, the Chilean Environmental Protection Agency.
Defensores des Bosque Chileno
Diagonal Oriente 1413
Ñuñoa- Santiago, Chile
Tel: 56.2.2041914
Fax: 56.2.2092527
Web site: www.elbosquechileno.cl

Selma James is the founder of the Wages for Housework Campaign and author of numerous books.
Wages for Housework Campaign
Crossroads Women's Centre
230A Kentish Town Rd.
London, England

Tel: (0) 207 482 2496
E-mail: crossroadswomenscenre@ compuserve.com

Chatsumarn Kabilsingh is a teacher and Buddhist activist who heads the women's temple, the Home of Peace and Love, near Bangkok, Thailand.
Home of Peace and Love
Songdharmakalyani Temple
195 Petkasem Hwy
Muang Dist., Nakhonpathom 73000

Käthe Kollwitz is a member of the Guerrilla Girls, activists who create performance art to bring attention to discrimination against women in the arts.
Web site: www.guerrillagirls.com/
E-mail: kathe@guerrillagirls.com

Dr. Olayinka Koso-Thomas is a medical doctor by profession and a public health consultant to international and national NGOs. She is vice-president of the Inter-African Committee on Traditional Practices Affecting the Health of Women and Children, and president of the Sierre Leone National Committee.
Inter-African Committee
145, rue de Lausanne
1202 Geneva,
Switzerland
Tel: 41-22-731220
Fax: 41-22-7381823
Web site: www.iac-ciaf.ch/

Sharon Labchuk is an environmental activist and member of the Earth Action Group in Prince Edward Island, Canada.
Candians Against Pesticides
Web site: www.caps.20m.com

Emily Lau is a political activist living in Hong Kong. She represents the geographical constituency of New Territories East in the 60-seat Hong Kong legislature (Legislative Council).
Web site: www.emilylau.org.hk

Joanna Manning is a feminist theologian and author. She lives in Toronto, Canada.
Catholics For A Free Choice (Canada)
14 Denison Square
Toronto, On, M5T 1K8
Tel: 416-599-1244
E-mail: jmanning@sympatico.ca

Monica McWilams is a university professor, and co-founder and member of the Northern Ireland Women's Coalition.
Web site: www.niwc.org/

Valentina Melnikova heads the Moscow branch of the Committee of the Soldiers' Mothers of Russia.
Luchnikov pereulok 4
Entrance 3, Room 5
101000 Moscow
Tel: (095) 9282506
Fax: (095) 2068958

An award-winning poet, novelist, political theorist, feminist activist, journalist, and editor, **Robin Morgan** has published more than a dozen books. Her most recent book is *Sisterhood Is Forever* (forthcoming Random House/Anchor, 2003). She is founder of the Sisterhood Is Global Institute.
E-mail: RMGeneral@aol.com

Zodwa Mqadi founded Agape Child Care Centre, an orphanage in Waterfall, South Africa, for children abandoned by AIDS.
PO Box 1528,
Linkhills, Durban
South Africa

Priscilla Nangurai is an educator and principal of the African Inland Church Girls' Primary Boarding School in Kajiado, Kenya. The school harbours girls who have escaped from arranged marriages.
P.O. Box 391
Kajiado, Kenya
Tel: (0301) 21033

Tandaswa Ndita is a magistrate and advocate for women's rights in the region around Mount Frere, Eastern Cape Province, South Africa.
Tel: 039-255-0251 or 039-255-0014

Chief Bisi Ogunleye is head of the Country Women's Association of Nigeria in Idoani, Nigeria, and is also a vice president of the Women's Environment and Development Organization.
Web site: www.wedo.org

Sebastiana Pantó Pox is part of the Ruth and Nohemi Co-operative of women weavers in Chontala, Guatemala.
c/o Ruth and Nohemi Cooperative
Centro de Iglesias, Sister Parish Centre
E-mail: spcenter@sisterparish.org

Kim Pate is executive director of the Canadian Association of Elizabeth Fry Societies, working on behalf of women in the justice system and women in conflict with the law.
Web site: www.elizabethfry.ca

Medha Patkar is a poverty and environmental activist, working with the Narmada Bachao Andolan, to save the Narmada River valley. She has also helped establish a network of activists across the country: the National Alliance of People's Movements.
Narmada Bachao Andolan
B-13, Shivam Flats, Ellora Park Road
Baroda, India 390 007

Tel: +91.265.28.22.32
Web site: www.narmada.org
E-mail: nba@lwbdq.lwbbs.net

Angela Bailōn Pérez heads UPAVIM, meaning United to Live Better, a cooperative program on the outskirts of Guatemala City.
Web site: www.upavim.org/

Rosa Tarlovsky de Riosinblit and Berta Shubaroff are founding members of the Grandmothers of the Plaza de Mayo.
Av. Corrientes 3281-4th H
1193 Capital Federal
Buenos Aires, Argentina
Tel: 54 (01) 864-3475 or 867-1212
E-mail: abuelas@wamani.ap.org
Web site: www.abuelas.org.ar/

Zainab Salbi is the founder of Women for Women International
725 K Street NW
Washington, D.C. 20037
E-mail: zsalbi@womenforwomen.org

Vandana Shiva is the founder of eco-feminism and one of the world's leading campaigners against the devastating human and environmental impacts of corporate-engineered international trade agreements.
A-60 Haus Khas, New Delhi-16
Tel: 0091-11-651-5003
Fax: 0091-11-685-6795
E-mail: vshiva@giasd101.vsnl.net.in

Long-time activist **Siriporn Skrobanek** heads the Foundation for Women in Bangkok, Thailand.
Foundation For Women
35/267 Charansanitwongse Road 62,
Soi Wat Paorohit,
Bangkoknoi, Bangkok 10700.
Thailand
E-mail: FFW@mozart.inet.co.th

Enakshi Ganguly Thukral is a social worker who is currently the executive director of HAQ: Centre for Child Rights, New Delhi. She has been working on issues of child rights and gender justice for over 15 years.
HAQ Centre for Child Rights
208 Shanpur Jat, New Delhi 110049
Tel: 00 91 11 6190306
Fax: 00 91 11 6192551
E-mail: haqcrc@vsnl.net

Mama Toribia, native elder and healer, lives in Ayacucho, Peru. She may be contacted c/o:
CHIRIPAQ, Centre of Indian Cultures
Horacio Urteaga 534
Oficina 203
11 Lima, Peru
E-mail: chirapaq@amauta.rep.net

Anastasia Posadskaya-Vanderbeck is director of the Network Women's Program, Open Society Institute, based in Budapest, Hungary.
400 West 59th Street, New York 10019
Tel: 212-548-0162
Fax: 212-548-4600
E-mail women@sorosny.org
oposadskaya@sorosny.org

Land-mines activist **Jody Williams** won the Nobel Peace Prize in 1997. She is based in Alexandria, Virginia, U.S.A.

Meilin Wu is a member of the Hong Kong Women Workers Association based in Kowloon, Hong Kong.
G/F, Tsui Ying House, Tsui Ping Estate
Kwun Tong, Kowloon
Tel.: 2790 4848
Fax: 2790 4922
E-mail: hkwwa@super.net.com

About the Authors

Nance Ackerman is a photojournalist whose work has been featured in *Time*, *Maclean's* and *Canadian Geographic*. Her photographs of First Nations women have been exhibited at the Museum of Civilization in Ottawa, Ontario and in a travelling exhibit sponsored by the APERTURE Foundation in the United States. She also freelances for the Smithsonian Institution, documenting Indigenous cultures for the National Museum of the American Indian. Nance lives in Nova Scotia with her two children.

Donna Nebenzahl is a columnist and feature writer at the *Montreal Gazette*, where in 1995 she launched "Woman News," a section devoted to women's issues. A freelance magazine writer who also teaches journalism at Concordia University in Montreal, Donna is the founder of Calling All Girls!, an annual forum for girls between the ages of nine and fifteen. She lives in Montreal, Canada, with her husband and two children.